Keep on Laughing

John E. Walker

Printed by:
A & J Printing
P.O. Box 518
Nixa, MO 65714

Published by and order from:
John A. Walker
530 Alger Ave.
Manistique, MI 49854
Phone: 906-341-2082

Library of Congress Cataloging-In-Publication Data
Walker, John A.

ISBN 0-9639798-0-9

3rd Printing

John A. Walker writes for:
White Pine Publishing Inc.
212 Walnut St.
Manistique, MI 49854
Phone: 906-341-5200
(Manistique Pioneer Tribune)

I dedicate this book to my mom and dad,
who really cared and showed it.

The U.P.
Upper Michigan

Lake Superior

Ontonagon

Area I Worked
District IV
Area 7

Canada

COPPER
COUNTRY

Wisconsin

Manistique

Lake Huron

Lake Michigan

300 miles north of Milwaukee

Northern
Michigan

300 Miles from Manistique to Lansing

First work
station

Down State

Lansing(capital)

A-1

INDEX

THE COVER

The picture of the deer on the cover of this book came from an old picture that was taken back in the mid-seventies. This buck was killed illegally, shot after the close of firearm deer season by poachers. This crew had tried all season long to get this buck at night with the aid of a spotlight, but could not get close enough to it for a shot. Instead they had to shoot it during the day, and we received a tip on their activity.

This buck had over twenty points and a spread of thirty some inches. In the picture it was sitting on the back of my patrol car.

This was the only time in my twenty-five years of service, as a Game Warden, that, after tracking a crew dragging an illegal deer, all I saw when I first observed the deer was antlers. I had never seen a rack like this before.

It was the biggest set of antlers on a buck killed illegally, I have ever observed, even to this day. The funny part was that the deer itself only went about 170 pounds ! I will tell the whole story about this deer later on, it is not in this book.

Conservation Officer's Stories
Upper Michigan Tales from a Game Warden's Perspective

"A DEER GETS REVENGE"

Forward:

The name of this book may be kind of misleading, because what started out to be a weekly Fish Report in the local paper turned into tales from a U.P. (Michigan's Upper Peninsula) Game Warden. It kind of became a weekly story about working as a Game Warden and growing up in God's Country, Michigan's U.P.

Growing up during the 40's and 50's in Ontonagon, a town in the Western part of the U.P., it seemed that a boy had his own little world built around his little U.P. town, his family, and the great outdoors. The rest of the world was so far off that you never gave a whole lot of thought to it. Back then there was no TV, and the radio would only pick up stations at night from places so far away that a boy could only dream about them. His heroes were his parents and grandparents. His best buddies were his brothers and a buddy from just down the block. Sisters were something a brother just had to put up with, made to tell dad what a brother did that he wished Dad never found out about, or just to have around to scare the fire out of. Usually you did this just to see what effect the "Discoveries" you came across out in the woods had on girls.

One thing you will notice about this book is that there are not any "bad" words used in it. Maybe some bad English, but not any bad words. For you see I grew up in the era of a bar of Fels-Naptha soap for boys if you used one of these words that are so common on TV and in everyday life today. I wanted something that even young kids could sit, read, and get a laugh out of without having to hide it between the box springs and mattress of their bed. Besides, I still have bad dreams of that dull red, green and dirty white soap wrapper when those words slipped out around Mom or Dad.

I guess you would say that I got to live the life my dad always dreamed of. You see, my dad quit school to be a fireman on a logging train. In fact when I got my job as a Michigan Conservation Officer, I had the job my Dad would have liked to have had. That's why he steered me towards it.

By listening to Dad and doing what he suggested, things fell into place for me. I spent a happy twenty-five years working as a Game Warden. A lot of these stories are those things that really happen to a Game Warden who is out in the field doing his job. Others are those passed down from officer to officer, plus those from hunter to hunter, that I heard during visits to hunting camps. Others are about growing up. Everyone likes to tell their favorite Game Warden story, "Their side of the Story."

Believe It ! All the facts are true, but they may just be dressed up with a little U.P. English, so you can better understand them. As some of the stories will tell, there are really three sides to every story. How the person involved saw it, how the Game Warden saw it, and the real truth as told in the bar to cover up getting caught. This we will call the middle ground. Could this be how other sportsmen would see it if their "buddy" was the one involved ?

Chapter 1

Attack Fisherman

Back in the mid-60's, the state of Michigan planted salmon in the Great Lakes to improve the sport fishing. You take an area where there are two of the Great Lakes, Michigan and Superior, 340 inland lakes, and 734 miles of streams, there you will find a lot of fish spawning areas. More than two or three Game Wardens can keep an eye on. When you have these spawning areas, with so few officers to watch them, in the spring and the fall of the year you will also have people who will be after the spawning fish. I think there are very few sport fishermen who ever saw anything like the first few salmon runs that we had. These creeks running out of the Great Lakes were packed from bank to bank with fish, three or four fish deep at times. I have observed men walk down to the edge of a creek in the dark, take a dip into the creek with a big landing net, and break the handle off the net trying to lift the fish out when it was so full.

When the fish get this heavy in a stream, you will always have those that think taking them by hook and line is too slow, so they try a different way. Here are a couple of stories about people after these salmon when the fish runs were so heavy.

There's Always A Way:

About the time that the salmon runs were really heavy for the first time out of the big lake, I had a new officer come to work with me. There was one spot where we had a real problem with people trying to take these salmon illegally. Now in this one area, there was a little bay, off this bay was a little cove in front of a bunch of cabins. Out in front of these cabins there were about a dozen docks going out into the cove. These docks were from fifteen to twenty feet long. The attack fishermen would go out on these docks to snag the salmon with big weighted hooks. (Under the sport fishing law in Michigan, you have to use a certain size hook, 3/8" from point to shank, also the fish must take the hook in its mouth to be a legally caught fish.)

Well, right after dark (it seems most of these people that take fish illegally like to do it under cover of darkness), you would see people on the attack. They would move out from between the cabins, down to the cove, and slip out on the docks to try to snag the fish that were spawning there. Afterwards, they would run back to hide their illegal fish near the cabins. After we found out about this problem and made plans to work it, we found us a hiding place near one of the cabins. From this vantage point we could watch the area of the cove where the docks were.

On this night, once we were in place, it began to look like ants on the move. The fishermen came from between the cabins down to the docks. We watched as a crew fishing on one of the docks took a couple of fish illegally and hid them. Although, by their actions, they looked to be using illegal hooks and methods to take their fish, we had a problem. You see, in the time we were watching this one crew, fifteen or twenty other fishermen had come out on the docks to fish. From their actions on the docks, you knew that 90% of them were all doing it the same way, ILLEGALLY !!

I told my new partner, "I really don't know what to do. There are fifteen to twenty people out on the docks now. If we jump this one crew and, the other fishermen don't like the idea, we have a serious problem on our hand - our well being !!"

In this area where we were working, there was not another law enforcement agency anywhere close by to help us out. In most cases it is this way where a Game Wardens work. They are usually on their own to look out for themselves. No help is nearby, so if you get in over your head, you just may get it knocked off.

After a few minutes of thinking things out, I told my partner to keep an eye on the crew of fishermen that had hid the fish. I ran back to my patrol car to get a little instamatic camera.

This was the type camera that took a little, square, four place flashbulb. When I got back, we both stepped out on the dock coming up behind the crew we wanted to catch. I yelled, "Conservation Office! Don't anybody move !" They all jumped around to look at us. At the same time, I held up the camera and flashed all four of the flashes as quick as they would go off right at the fishermen standing out on the dock with shocked faces. Nobody moved! After we issued our tickets to those that had taken the illegal fish, we left.

For years after in that area, we would attend meetings and hear about the new officer who had moved into the area and used an infrared camera to put a stop to the illegal fishing off the docks in that cove.

By the way, in case you don't know it, if you take a picture with a 110 instamatic camera in the pitch dark, all that shows up is the flash going off, not a picture of the fishermen in shock standing out on the dock.

Sounds In The Night:

The same new officer and I were working on an illegal gill net case right down the shore from the cove sometime later. We had located a box of gill nets hidden along the shore in the brush while working the salmon runs. We watched this area night after night with no luck. We knew where they had been setting the nets for salmon, where their fish house was located, but we could never catch them in the act of using the gill nets. We made it a practice to check this area whenever we went by it on patrol. You see, we had to hide the patrol car, then we would walk into the area of the fish house to check it out for any illegal activity.

One night when we were working together, I had made plans to stay at this officer's house because we had to work at the state park early the next morning. We patrolled around that evening, ending up in the area where the illegal gill netting was taking place. We thought we might as well hide the patrol car and walk into the fish house. It was midnight or later by this time, we walked in and found a pickup truck parked near the fish house. This was the first time we had ever found a vehicle here. We spent some time looking around, but we could not find anybody in the area. After a while, we thought that maybe the pickup had just been dropped off at the fish house to be used later. We walked out to the patrol car and returned home for the night.

About 2:30am, we were having a cup of coffee at his house when at the same time we both said, "We ought to check out that pickup again."We laughed because we both had the same idea at the same time. Things just did not seem normal back in the area where the truck had been left. We got back into our uniforms and drove back to the area where we had observed the pickup.

After we hid the patrol car, we walked back into the fish house. A good Game Warden does all his walking around in the dark of the night without the aid of any flashlight. You really get used to moving around in the dark because you do not want anyone to know where you are or that you are around. We got to the area of the fish shed. All of a sudden, we could hear the sound of lead weights hitting the bottom of a boat out in the bay. We hid. You want to remember that any illegal fishermen worth his salt does all his illegal activity without the aid of a flashlight, also. We could not see a thing, but every now and then, we could hear a noise from them out on the lake. Now, you have these two groups of people running around in the dark without lights, one group now knowing the other group is there, but hoping the others do not know they are there.

We listened to their boat return to shore, and we watched as the door of the fish house opened. Boxes of nets were carried from the boat to the fish house. Although we could see the shadows of people moving around, the people going to and from the boat and fish house, we could not tell how many bodies were involved. We tried to figure out from their actions how many men were there, but it was too dark. They finally finished up outside, and all went into the fish house and closed the door.

Now we had our crew of illegal gill netters in the fish house but no idea how many people were in there. We were also on our own because this area was back out of the way. Any other law enforcement agency would be miles away and need time to get to our aid. If we ended up needing help now, there was not any to be had.

We put our two outstanding minds to work. We figured that this time of night, 3:00am in the morning, the hard work that gill netting was, plus carrying all those heavy boxes around, it had to be quite a crew of strong young men. This gill netting activity was an easy way to make a fast buck, so adding everything up, we knew what we had to look forward to.

We finally decided the best way to do it. We would hit them hard and fast, hoping to take them by complete surprise, therefore taking them all before they knew there were only two of us. Both of us are over six feet tall. We weigh on the plus side of 200 pounds. Our plan was all set.

Let your mind work. It is 3:30 in the morning, out in the middle of nowhere, dark as can be outside, when all of a sudden, the door of your fish house goes sailing off its hinges flying across the room. (It was not as strong as we figured.) Into the opening jump two 200 pound green giants yelling, "Don't anybody move! Stop right there !!"

What did we find ?

Two old men in their 70's (now under cardiac arrest instead of our arrest). wondering where their fish house door had gone, and if someone from outer space had landed on top of them !

Now this "Big Arrest" of some of the first people caught taking salmon with illegal gill nets in Michigan made the big city newspapers, but you now know the real story.

Chapter 2

BEFORE 45

A while back (This phrase could mean any time from birth to death), one of my boys called home from college and said he had to do a report about the history of the 60's. Now that is 1960 ! I told him, "That wasn't history ! It's when your Dad says,("You know the other day.....)"

Maybe he's not the only one that thinks that my mind belongs in history books. You see, one day the following article came across my desk. I don't know who thought it up or wrote it, but it is true. I thought I would pass it on.

"For Those Born Before 1945"

WE ARE SURVIVORS !!!....Consider the changes we have witnessed.

We were born before TV, before penicillin, before the polio shot, frozen foods, Xerox, plastic, contact lenses, frisbees, and the pill. We were before radar, credit cards, split atoms, laser beams, and the ballpoint pens. Before panty hose, dishwashers, clothes dryers, electric blankets, air conditioners, drip-dry clothes... and before men walked on the moon.

We got married first and "then" lived together. How quaint can you be ! In our time, closets were for clothes, not for "coming out of". Bunnies were small rabbits, and Rabbits were not Volkswagons. Designer Jeans were scheming girls named Jean, and having a meaningful relationship meant getting along with your cousins.

We thought "fast food" was what you ate during Lent, and outer space was back of the movie theater. We were before house husbands, gay rights, computer dating, dual careers, and commuter marriages. We were before "day-care" centers, group therapy, and nursing homes. We never heard of FM radios, tape decks, CD players, electronic typewriters, artificial hearts, word processors, yogurt, and guys wearing earrings. For us, time-sharing meant togetherness... not computers or condominiums, a chip was a piece of wood, hardware meant hardware, and software was not even a word !

Back then, "made in Japan" was JUNK, and the term "making out" referred to how you did on your final exam. Pizza, McDonald's, and instant coffees were unheard of. We hit the scene when there were "5 and 10 cent stores", where you bought things for a nickel or a dime. For a nickel, you could see a movie with a friend and have a treat, make a phone call, have a Pepsi, or buy enough stamps to mail a letter and two post cards. You could buy a Chevy coupe for $600.00.. But who could afford one ? A pity, too, for gas was 11 cents a gallon.

In our day, grass was mowed, coke was a soft drink, and pot was something Mom cooked in. Rock music was Grandma's lullaby, and aids were helpers in the principal's office. We were certainly not before the difference between the sexes was discovered but were surely before the sex change. We made do with what we had, and we were the last generation that was so dumb as to think you needed a husband to have a baby.

No wonder we are so confused, and there is such a generation gap today, and we are so misunderstood !! But we have survived !!!!!!! What better reason to stand up and cheer !!

Chapter 3

COOK'S NIGHT HUNT

Well, I am going to tell you one of my favorite Game Warden stories. First, let me tell you about Cooks. This is a little town in the corner of Schoolcraft County, so that it kind of sits out of the way for Game Wardens from either Schoolcraft or Delta County to work on a regular basies. For this reason the people of Cooks for years just took it upon themselves to make good use of any deer that happened to wander through their area. For years we received very few complaints or tips from this area on illegal hunting, but when we did they were usually a good one.

One day, a lady from the Cooks area came up to me in the county courthouse to tell me that there was a lot of illegal night hunting for deer going on near her place. It was an old apple orchard behind Cooks. Now there are a good number of trees there where an old farm used to be. There were only 2-track roads going to and from the area of the orchard. The violators could take one out of Cooks, travel through some old fields, and never have to come out on a main road all the time they were looking for deer. She stated that some of the night hunters were some of the local boys and that it was going on almost every night for the past week. I made plans with the other local Game Warden, a new officer, to work the area of the Cooks orchard that night.

We met as planned and went out that night to a hill that over looks Cooks. It is called Sobieski's Hill. Here we took a right turn down a gravel road toward the area of the orchard. Now you want to remember that back in those days we drove all over while on patrol at night without ever using our headlites. It was just the way things were done back then to help give you a little advantage in trying to get up on the violators. We came down this gravel road, and all of a sudden we saw headlights out in a field off to our right !! We shut the patrol car off and got out to listen. We could hear a couple of people talking, but could not tell what they were saying. Then we heard a thump like something thrown in the bed of a pickup, then heard the tailgate being closed. The vehicle then started moving out of the field toward our road. We took the patrol car and parked cross-ways of the road to block it off. The vehicle came out of the field about 100 feet down the road from us, then turned toward us. At this point for the first time we turned on the patrol car lights- the headlights, plus the blue light on top the car and the spotlights. The people in the pickup just floored it !! Off they went into a deep ditch right in front of us, then back up on the road, then just took off.

We jumped into the patrol unit to take off after them back over Sobieski's hill. We were chasing a Chevy pickup with two guys in it. Down the gravel road, across the blacktop road going into Cooks, and down the gravel road for another two miles. All of a sudden the driver of the pickup took a hard left turn through the ditch, out into an old field. As he bounced through the ditch, a six point buck went flying up in the air to land right in front of the patrol car ! I went around it and off after them again. Now there was no way I was going to let them get away !!

I now knew what they were trying to do ! That was to get out in an area called the Thompson Plains.

On these plains, there are miles of 2-track roads and sand hills. They were in a pickup and I was in a car, so here they would try to lose us. Both vehicles went across a forty-acre field and came up to an old three strand barb wire fence. He drove right through it ! and I followed him. All of a sudden, he realized he had turned off the road to quick !! Right in front of them was this big rock wall, running all the way from the woods back out to the road. This is where for years the farmers had dumped the rocks they picked up in the fields to get rid of them. This wall was at least four feet high and there was no way through it. The driver turned to the left so quick that he ran into a big White Pine tree. Hitting it so hard that he snapped the top right out of it and left his running lights stuck in the tree. Their vehicle bounced off the tree, doing damage to the passenger side of the truck. Now they made a left hand circle around the field. After seeing the the rock fence and their turn to the left, I went in a circle opposite the way they were going with the intent of hitting them head-on to try and stop them. Spinning through the muddy field, we were not going that fast. We came toward each other, but at the last minute he took a hard right and I took a hard left hand turn ! The driver of the truck and the officer on the passenger side of the patrol car could have reached out and shook hands if they had wanted to. Things were rather close. They now made a right hand circle, and I made a left hander to get back in behind them. We were now both heading back toward the gravel road, me with the window washers trying to keep the mud off the window so I could see where I was going. Back through the barb wire fence we went again and across the forty-acre field. All this time we were running in and out of ground fog that would keep you from seeing the ground in front of you. All of a sudden the pickup in front of us went airborne !! cleared the whole width of the gravel road and then some, and landed on its grill way beyond the ditch on the other side of the road! The new officer with me for the last part of the trip kept yelling, "We'll be killed !! We'll be killed !!" Me, I thought that all Game Wardens always drove this way. It was the way I had been taught.

After their pickup landed on its grill, it twisted around and came to a rest back on its wheels. The chase was over. The truck had twisted so much that the back window came flying out. While the two in the truck were still in a daze and doing an after flite check out, we came up to their vehicle to place them under arrest. We were standing there talking to them about our adventure when one of them looked over and Yelled, "Your cars on fire !" All four of us ran over and I backed up the patrol car so we could beat out the fire that had started under it from the hot exhaust. When the fire was out, we finished our talk with them then took them off to jail.

You see up here they go out after their illegal deer, try their best not to get caught or to get away if they are caught, but the funny thing is most of us all know each other from times before. We did go back and pick up the buck.

Chapter 4

DEER HUNTERS

Well, the day that all those funny looking guys in the bright orange suits have been waiting for is almost upon us. I cannot believe the change in the hunters from the "90s" compared to the hunters of the "40s". Now this article is about the "now-a-day" hunters of the "90s".

First I cannot believe all the "deer bait" that I have observed being brought up to the U.P. in trucks and by the trailer load. As these hunter's trek to their special hunting spot. Things that farmers could not give away a few years back and had to haul back out in the field to plow under, they now put in a bag and call it "deer bait" to sell to those funny guys in the bright orange suits. Now, let your mind stop working, than couldn't you just picture this ? Just think what we must look like to a couple of people from another planet that happened to drift over the U.P. around the 15th of November, around the start of Michigan's firearm deer season. This couple from planet X are watching, than have to return to their planet to report to their boss what they saw on their trip down here to earth.

First of all, to get everything in it's proper context, you have to remember that we think we are the most squared away group of beings in our whole solar system. Better yet, picture this, this guy and his buddy down here on earth, naturally from lower Michigan, have been planning this trip to the U.P. to deer hunt for a year now. The time to get ready finally comes.

First of all this guy has to go out and get his vehicle ready. He lives down in the "blacktop jungle", but you have to own a big 4x4, with big tires and a roll bar with twenty-seven lights to make that that once a year hunting trip to deer camp. (deer camp sits on a blacktop road.) The rest of the year you just get to listen to the tires sing as you drive on the pavment. His truck is all set, so they start to load it. They load all there hunting junk into the pickup until there is no room to sit or move. In fact things are so tight they have to take turns breathing for the whole trip. But from the looks of it they should have all they need. plus all they might need if any of those thousand of things that can go wrong on a hunting trip turn up to go wrong. You always want to be prepared. But deep deep down they really know that 2/3 of what they now have packed and are taking they would never use in a million hunting trips, but there is always that chance. Now lets see:

There is the 3-wheeler, in case it dosen't snow, then the snowmobile, in case it does. There are all the clothes for warm weather, plus all those for the cold weather, the dry weather, plus the wet weather. There are a different pair of boots for sitting, hiking, the swamp, the marsh, plus the really cold weather and the not so cold weather. All this plus their camp supplies are in the truck or on the trailer hooked behind the truck for the snowmobiles and ATV,s. Then they try to squeeze into the cab with all the things they cannot let freeze or get cold for their trip to the U.P.

All set, so they head up I-75 for the U.P., but just a couple miles down the road they see this big pile of sugar beets that some Bay City farmer could not get into the sugar factory, so he put then out next to the road with a big sign that reads "deer bait". Our two hunters know a good deal when they see it, so they stop and buy about half a ton of sugar beets which they throw on top the trailer between the snowmachines and ORVs. Off we go again. With all this load and a 4x4 another hundred miles down the road they have to stop for gas. Here they find that this gas station also has a sideline, big bags of carrots for "deer bait" that the owner of the gas station is almost giving away to the deer hunters that stop for gas. So a half dozen bags go onto the trailer on top of the sugar beets. North they go now almost to the Mackinac Bridge, when they stop for coffee and would you believe it find a pickup truck parked there selling of all things "deer apples". So onto the trailer on top of the carrots, which are on top of the sugar beets, which rest on a couple snowmachines and ORVs go about three hundred pounds of "deer apples". Off we go again. But it's gas up time again, for there is nothing open between St. Ignace and Manistique this time of night. Look !! Over there! bags of "deer corn" !! So you guessed it, up on the load go a few bags of corn. By now they are at least across the Mackinac Bridge going West on US-2 through God's country the U.P. They hit Naubinway and see there is a coffee shop open and stop for a refill to help keep them awake for they final dash to deer camp. But here they find a big pile of pumpkins that are really cheap seeing they never sold for halloween. On top the load go a few of these.

They are now making good time, for there is nothing to stop at on US-2 at 2:00am in the morning on this stretch. They are just East of Blaney

Park (2:00am), which is 50 miles from "no where" this time of night, when they blow a tire right off their trailer, could this be from being way over the load limit on their trailer tires ?

Guess where the jack and the spare tire for the trailer are ? Right !! Under the pumpkins, which sit on the bags of corn, which rest on the apples, which sit on the sugar beets and the snowmobiles and ATVs. No, the spare tire is there, but the jack is in the back of the truck under all the camping gear, the hunting equipment and the food.

Finally, they get to deer camp, the area of the big hunt. They have read all the good reports in the down state papers about this years deer season, along with this secret spot being on a TV outdoor show, plus in six hunting magazines.

Now remember that we are looking at these two hunters through the eyes of our friends sent here from planet X to check up on how we do thing. They are watching and filling out their reports to take back to their boss when they return. But the best is yet to come.

After sleeping in their truck, for they did not have time to set up camp, these two guys get out of their pickup, they then put on these bright orange suits, and take a couple of 5-gallon buckets to fill up with "deer bait". Now you want to put a little of everything in your bucket and just the right amount. You see it is like a salad bar set up for the deer. They get just the right portions in each bucket, then they go off sneaking through the woods in bright orange suits hoping nobody will see where they go to. For you see they figure if they saw all the articles on the deer hunting in this area, so did half a million other Michigan deer hunters. So they, too, know about this secret spot. They finally find their perfect spot with a lot of deer sign, both rubs and scrapes. Looking around they figure that the last person in this spot was Ward Bond when he went through the area with Wagon Train. They dump their "deer Bait" and build a couple of good blinds up on the ridge over-looking the bait pile.

They now go back to camp and spend half the night getting things set up and put away. The next morning each guy is up way before daybreak, putting on his longies, his electric socks, his sweater, felt lined boots, his wool hunting pants, and over this his bright orange suit. Then with his rifle and two bait buckets he sneaks off for his deer blind so he will be there well before daylight. Sweating like a mule all the way for it is up in the fifties this openning day morning. He dumps his bait and crawles into his deer blind ringing wet from the walk in with all these clothes on.

Nothing to do now but just sit and wait for daylight. As daylight comes, this couple from planet X look down, here is this guy in the bright orange suit so warm, so tired, so comfortable... he is sound asleep sitting in a brush pile ! While a big ten point buck is having a super breakfast on all the different types of bait he carried in that morning and dumped, unkown to our hunter whose sound asleep !! Now, how would you like to be these two guys that have to go back to tell their boss about the intelligent life that lives down here on earth ?

P.S. Don't worry about our hunter, because he forgot his hunting license.. back home..on the kitchen table. so he does not have a deer tag with him anyway

Chapter 5

SOMETHING NEW

Well, I have to sit here and laugh about things in today's day and age. If it is not brand new, in style, who wants it ? My kids would say, "We know dad ! back when you were a kid, you walked up hill both to and from school, through six foot deep snow all year around, HA !!" But it's true that back when I was a kid, you really never knew what "store bought" things were. As my good U.P. Mom used to say, "Someday the Good Lord is going to make this country pay for all the good things they waste." What that meant in her terms was that you handed things down from kid to kid till they were wore out, but even then if it still had some life in it you never would even think of throwing it away, but passed it on to another family with younger kids then yours. Then, after it was really worn out you took off all the buttons and snaps and used the material that was left to patch the hand-me-downs you were still wearing.

It was just the way life was back then, everyone lived that way, didn't they ?

SURE SIGN OF MANHOOD:

Back yonder in the good old days, for you kids, it was not really that long ago there were electric lights, (but I could show you where the electric power line ended and those that never had it yet) indoor plumbing, (in town) airplanes and motor cars ! (But there were no state speed limits once outside of the town limits) I can still sit here thinking back to some of the special days. Like just before the Fall season, when a boy had just turned eleven years old. This meant that this year he got to really go hunting with Dad. No more "Red Ryder" BB guns for you, now a real hand-me-down single shot 20 gauge, that had been Dads first gun also. Now you were really going to get to hunt birds. August had went by and October 1st was here the big day. Dad and Grandpa called you in and said, " We have something for you." Then they gave you an old plaid (red and black) hunting shirt that one of them had worn. Mom had reworked it as best she could, fixed most the holes, and got it as best she could from a mans size to a boys. Later it may have been an old wool hunting coat for you to wear when out with Dad. It too had seen better days many years before, but who cared. A few holes never hurt a boy, now old enough to hunt, besides it had been Grandpa's coat. It had a lot of hunting history behind it and now you got to add to it, you hoped. Or maybe it was a special hunting cap that Grandma or Mom had knit. Boy, I have now arrived !

Now you do have to remember that by the time a boy got these special hunting clothes there was usually a reason for it. Like the elbows of the shirt were so badly worn out they could not be patched anymore, or the jacket had to many battle scares from the moth, or it had already been handed down through all those in the household that could wear it before it ever got to you. But who cared !! It was an honor, for those now old enough to hunt !! Now they were yours to wear ! Man ! A hunting coat ! Besides they were not really worn out, only broke in by some real hunters, your Dad and Grandpa, the real hunters of the family. It's funny, but back then even socks were patched up to be handed down. Mom would sit at night, with a glass in a sock and yarn, doing the one job she had no love for. She sure let us know it too when our socks got holes in them. I guess it was when I was in the army that I found out that the bumps on the back of socks were for your heels, not the calves of your legs.

GIRL'S NEW DRESSES:

For some reason girls did not see the same value in hand-me-downs that a boy did. Maybe it was because hunting was really something they could take or leave, while with a boy it was really important. For this reason, here in the U.P., Mom had a way of getting something "new" for the girls. There was no way dresses from mom or Grandma could be handed down to the girls, so she would make plans way ahead of time to visit the local Co-op store. You see, you had to be on the ball when the new shipment of flour came in. Back then flour came in cloth sacks with patterns printed on them. I guess this was for girls only, because there were no hunting type patterns printed on them. For this reason Mom had to try and get matching sacks in order to get enough material to make dresses. Somehow or other, through trading sacks with others or the help of the people that ran the Co-op store, Mom always came through with a new dress for the girls. I cannot see how wearing flour sacks was something special when real clothes, with class, were handed down from Grandpa with the smell of hunting camp still in them, for a boy to use while learning to hunt.

HAND-ME-DOWN-HOUSES:

Back in those days everything was hand-me-downs, even in some cases houses. My Mom and Dad bought their house for $250.00 from the Conservation Department. They were sure proud of it, it was a place to call their own. Some people made due with even a less of a start then we did.

A couple of us were talking about this subject of today's wants at coffee one day. About how "now days", so many young couples have to have everything all at once. Plus, it just has to be new ! It just seems to them that life is not treating them right if things they get are second hand. They need right away: a new car; his truck; a newer home; and all that goes with it, when they first start out together.

One of the older men at coffee told this story.

Denton and his wife were living in an apartment when they first got married. He owned a logging truck, hauling logs for a living. Friends kept telling them that they ought to buy a house rather then throw their money away on rent, but he could not afford one. Who could afford a home back then ?

Back then, logging off areas was done differently then it is today. (But aren't most things ?) Buildings were set up at the logging site to make up a logging camp. Bunk houses and a cook shack. The area where Denton was working was now logged off and plans were made to move off to a new stand of timber. Usually the crew would take all the buildings down, load them on the trucks, and take them off to the site of the next camp. This time things went a little different as they made ready for the trip to the next job. This time it seemed that the old cook shack had come to the end of the line. The boss felt the cook shack had been moved from place to place once to often and it could not stand another move. After looking it over and seeing what shape it was in it was decided to leave it where it was and replace it at the new camp site.

The truck driver came up to the boss to tell him what he had overheard, that they were going to abandon the old cook shack. When the boss confirmed that they were going to leave it, he asked if he could have it. He was told that he could. One weekend he and his brothers took his logging truck, and they went up to dismantle the old cook shack, loaded it on his truck and moved it into town.(Manistique) He told me it looked like a real pile of junk on the back of his truck.

They took it to an empty lot where they built a foundation to set it up on. The four walls and roof that make up a logging camp cook shack. They then divided it up to make rooms. It became their first real home, they owned it and was really theirs ! Just think, your home for free, plus a lot of hard work !!

Now having known this man for almost twenty years, he is one of the happiest, most contented people you could ever meet. By the way, this couple that started out with a cook shack home raised a good crew of kids, plus some grand kids that come by now, never really knowing how this home got started.

I guess no matter what we do, the key to having a good time is to be really satisfied, to make up our minds to just be happy with what we have. I don't care if it's at home, out hunting or fishing or just doing everyday things. Some people always seem to have a great time in everything they do, while others always seem to think they got the short end of the stick or that they didn't get a fair shake. Thinking back to some of the best times you had, they were when you had the least, but never realized it for everyone else was in the same boat.

Chapter 6

EXTRACTORS

Thompson Creek, runs out of Lake Michigan about five miles West of Manistique. It is a small two-step creek where the Salmon and steelhead trout run in to spawn. Now when you have 12-14 pound steelhead sitting there in eight to ten inches of water, you are going to have those people that are going to try to extract them. I would hate to guess how many hours I spent lying along the side of this creek waiting for the extractors to come along. You want to remember that if a Conservation Officer is worth a hoot and going to do a good job catching a few crooked fishermen, he spends half his time or more running around in the dark without using any lights. It seems that there is a lot more that goes on under the cover of darkness. For this reason a Game Warden has to learn to walk along in the dark without using the flashlight he has with him. He just picks his way through the woods using only his feelings and the natural light that may be out there. Here are a couple of fish stories about working along Thompson Creek.

A LOVING WIFE:

We all know that in order to do his job a Game Warden has to have special help and special power. But, they would just as soon have it only on their terms, at the right time. Back a number of years ago a Game Warden had to supply a lot of his own equipment. We bought our own flashlights, waders, snowmobile suits, etc. These type items were bought by the officer himself, or his family would wait for his birthday or Christmas to buy him something he really needed. On this night I was working the Thompson Creek area with an officer that had come down from Grand Marais. When we got there and had hid out patrol car, he showed me what he had just received for his birthday. It was a new flashlight that his wife had bought him. This new flashlight took a brick type battery that would last for a long time when out working. He was really glad to get it. We went out to work, walking from our hid patrol car, along the banks of Thompson Creek. We walked through the woods to our hiding spot. Now in order for our plan to work just right and to get the extractors to try to remove the steelhead from the creek, you have to make sure that there is some "bait" in the creek. We had sat for a while with no activity, so we decided to check the creek to make sure there was some "bait" in it. The other officer was standing by the creek bank, using his new flashlight to see if any steelhead were spawning. All of a sudden, we heard someone coming through the woods along the creek. We quickly shut off our flashlights and hit the ground to hide. The people coming along the creek bank came closer and closer to the area where our bait" was, BUT all of a sudden they took off running through the woods away from us !! We could not figure out what in the world could have spooked them till we looked behind us. It seems that this Game Warden's loving wife-always looking out for his best interest did not want him to misplace his new flashlight in the dark, so she had given him one that glowed in the dark when you shut it off ! Needless to say this may be a great idea for almost all other people, but it is not for a Game Warden trying to hide in the dark.

RETRIEVING:

We were again working the area along Thompson Creek during the fall
Salmon runs. We had a good spot to hide that was near the weir. This is a
gate-like structure that is placed across the creek to stop the fish from
running farther up stream. We had made a number of good cases here,
because it is illegal to take fish from the area of the weir. Therefore we
were not surprised to see a party make his way down to the creek in the
dark. He did not seem to be carrying anything, but this was not really
unusual since a lot of extractors will have their illegal devices in their
pockets, spears hid along the creek, or just use their hands to grab the
fish in the shallow water. We watched as this party worked his way along
the bank of the creek to the mouth. All the time he was checking the
creek for fish along the way. We also saw that there was a dog walking
along with him. I was laying behind a log about twenty feet from the
creek, so I had a good view of both the party and his dog. The other
Game warden was right beside me. All of a sudden, he called the dog
over with a whistle and hand signals. He then sent him into the creek to
retrieve something. We lay there and watched as he got the dog, who was
really well trained, to bring three nice salmon up out of the creek. The
only problem was that the dog must have smelled us before he brought
the three fish over and laid them right on the other side of the log that we
were hiding behind. Finally, the party must have thought he had enough
fish, because he called off the dog and came over to get his fish—plus
the game Warden, too. It sure made news around town about the guy that
got a ticket for fishing with an illegal dog. See back then Thompson
Creek was closed to all kinds of fishing this time of year.

But the best part of the story is that years later I ran across this same guy.
He told me, "It wasn't even my dog I got caught with. I had just heard
about how good he was at getting fish, so I borrowed him that night to
get a few. and he really was good."

26

GRAB FIRST THINK LATER:

The main pastime for the youth of Thompson is to go down to Thompson Creek and get a couple of big steelhead. The only problem is they do not seem to outgrow it. Therefore, you run into a number of those in their twenties down after fish. I have never been fast on my feet, and as old age kept coming on I went from slow to much slower.

On this night, we hid our patrol car way down the road. We knew the locals would check all the normal hiding spots to see if we were around before hitting the creek to take some fish. The two of us were hiding down by the creek when we heard a car stop on the road across the field from the weir. I then heard a party call my name a number of times to see if I would answer. I knew he was up to no good for he kept calling for "Johnny Walker" and only violators call me "Johnny Walker". The "good guys" call me John Walker.

After a bit, we worked our way upstream along the creek to the area of the footbridge at Thompson. All of a sudden, against the lights of Thompson, I saw a person standing on the bridge. I figured he was the lookout for someone in the creek. We worked our way up along the tree line to the area of the bridge. We got as close as we figured we could without scaring them off. Then, all two hundred- and-some pounds of me went running out on this now bouncing bridge and grabbed this party in the dark as fast as I could. At the same time shining my flashlight, and that of my partners into the creek on another party standing there in shock with a spear in his hands with a big steelhead flopping on it.

7

CAN I HELP YOU ?

One fall a buddy of mine was up bear hunting from Tennessee. We decided to take a ride out to Thompson Creek, so he could see all the salmon spawning up against the weir. I was not working so I wore regular clothes and he had on his normal cowboy hat and boots. My wife and his boy were with us.

As we walked across the opening into the area of the weir, I saw a party down in the creek in front of the weir. When we got closer, I saw he had a landing net and was taking fish. He was placing them up in the woods on the far side of the weir. We walked out on the weir and the party came out of the trees and must have figured he had enough fish. He saw the five of us standing there (looking like real non-fishermen) and wanting to do what was right, came down with his net and asked if we wanted him to get us a few fish. My buddy could hardly keep a straight face as I told him "no-thanks" and walked over to look at his catch. He came over and showed them to us. Then I just had to go and ruin his day ! I told him who I was and showed him my ID. He just stood there shaking his head.

But he had a good sense of humor, because when he went to court to square up, he laughed about probably being the only guy to offer to help the Game Warden out in getting a few fish illegally, seeing he did not have any fishing gear with him.

Chapter 7

FLYING:

I hate to fly !!! Unless I am riding on something that touches the ground like a snowmobile, ORV, ATV, motorcycle, etc. I have flown in years gone by across the country a number of times, but I do not care for it anymore. In fact, one day I was with the boss at the Manistique airport. He stated that one of us ought to go up with the pilot in Air-4 as he flew out over Lake Michigan looking for illegal gill net tugs. I said, "Better you than me." So off the boss went with Air-4 up into the wild blue yonder. Spared from having to fly again !

But sometimes as you go through life you get into a spot where you cannot really back out of it when it comes up. We were working along with the Michigan State Police on a big forest fire investigation a few years back. During the course of this investigation there was a need to fly down to lower Michigan to interview a number of people. Now, if you have never been in Michigan's U.P., you have to remember that from some places in Michigan the Atlantic ocean is closer than going from the Northwest corner of the U.P. to the Southeast corner of the lower peninsula. For this reason the State Police decided to ask for their Department plane to fly us down state. Great !! Four of us were going to hook a ride out of Marquette in the U.P. down state to Lansing in lower Michigan.

We left our home town of Manistique to drive the ninety miles to Marquette and —- wouldn't you know it-it was snowing and blowing all the way to the Marquette airport. We got to the airport at

Marquette and met up with the men from the State Police. Then we waited for the airplane to arrive to pick us up. Now nobody wants to be thought of as a "wimp", so you just take a deep breath and hope the sweat does not show up through your jacket. At least you figure the odds are on your side. The plane that is to pick us up lands, it is a twin engine-eight passenger. The pilot, an older guy with a lot of gray hair, gets out. From the talk of the two State Police guys, you know this pilot has been around for a while, they say he is a good pilot, plus an all right guy. They have flown with him for years. Great, things are looking up. The other pilot with him is a younger guy. Now here I was with old age just twenty to thirty years away getting to do what I really did not want to do, and hoping that I would get the twenty or thirty years down the road to check out old age !!

The plane looked to be in good shape. It has an experienced pilot who I figured at least had his act together. Even if I still did not want to fly, he would be at the controls. It came time to leave and we went out and got into the plane. We placed our gear in the back and took our seats. Now in this style of plane there are not any secrets. The passengers sit right behind the pilot, and they can read all the gauges as well as the pilot can, plus hear and see everything that is going on.

The younger pilot gets in and takes his seat on the left. Then, the older, experienced pilot, takes his seat on the right. I am sitting directly behind the younger pilot. Now we were all set to go. BUT, the first sign that I had that things were not going exactly as I had them in my mind now came about. All of a sudden, I realized things were going to be interesting, I heard the old pilot telling the younger pilot how to start the plane !! Then how to fly it !! Just my luck !! I hate to fly !! Now here I go off into the wild blue yonder, into a snowstorm, out across Lake Michigan, with a pilot who is on his learners permit !! You have to realize that what makes matters all the worse, is that my daughter had just completed Driver's Training. She too had her learners permit saying she could drive (???), but at least with her I am on the ground.

We taxi out to the end of the runway as the older pilot tells his partner about the plane. Me and my icy, cold sweat that makes me feel like I am going to freeze to death. Can a person die of hypothermia from a cold sweat wondering if an airplane will get off the ground before they come to the end of the runway ? Then I hear the old pilot tell the "learner", "use a lot of power on the left engine, give it a lot more power then the right, this airport has a bad crosswind and it is hard to lift off of." OH MAN ! Just what I needed to hear. My cold sweat has turned to icebergs. Well, we got off with only a few bumps, almost like riding a snow machine across a frozen lake at 90 miles an hour. We went up to 15,000 feet over all the bad weather, where the rest of the trip was nice and smooth, well almost, remember you do have to come down. As we came down to 2,000 feet, the clouds were again all around us and it was snowing. Do you know how much a small plane will jump around in a storm while trying to line up on a runway that looks like a postage stamp? Or really how small this strip of runway looks out the front of a plane ? Well, we made it down with just some slipping and sliding. But thank goodness we took a car on our return trip back to the U.P.

Chapter 8

GAME WARDEN FOLLIES:

One thing that you can be sure of is that with all the hours a Game Warden spends out checking people, if something can go wrong, it usually will. I think each and every officer could tell you about a time they would just as soon forget ever happened. But as the years go by and the stories get told and retold, they just seem to get better with age. Not only that, but some of the stories, you just cannot ever let those involved forget they really happened.

Flipper:

One day, I was working with a young Conservation Officer who always looked as sharp as could be. This officer had been quite an athlete, and his pride in his appearance carried over into his job. On this day we had made plans to meet at the state police post before heading out to work. We met in the parking lot and walked into the post through the front door. As you come in the door, right off to the left is the Post Commander's office. We had no sooner entered the post through the door when the Lieutenant asked, "How's Flipper doing today ?" From the look on this young officer's face that was with me, I quickly knew there was something here that I did not know about. Seeing he was caught, the officer told his story to us at the post (with the help of the Post Commander).

It seems that a couple of days before, this officer was out on Indian Lake doing boat patrol, checking fishermen. He came up along the side of a boat holding a couple of men out fishing with their kids. Since the officer was working by himself, he had to be careful when pulling up to their boat with all the fishing lines hanging out over the side of the boat. Everything went all right, and he checked the adults for their fishing licenses and safety equipment for their boat. He talked to them a few minutes about the fishing on the lake and the best spots. The officer got ready to leave, pushed off, than put his boat motor in gear. At just the same second, he heard the whistle of a fishing reel and one of the kids yelled, "I got something !" The officer knew the boy had caught something all right - the prop on his patrol boat motor.

He shut off the motor and went to the back of the boat. Here, he reached over the back and tilted up the motor so he could see the prop. Sure enough, a line was wrapped around it. He leaned over the back to try to get the line untangled from around the bottom of the motor, reaching down and out from the boat. All of a sudden, just like life had moved into slow motion, like instant replay at a football game on TV, the boat motor settled back into the water, while the officer went out of sight over the back of the boat. He scored a perfect ten in the form he used while making this dive into Indian Lake, uniform and all.

Well, he got back into the boat after the line was untangled (it was easier to work on standing in the lake). The officer swore them all to secrecy.

They all promised never to tell a soul what had happened to the officer out on the lake, and they didn't, on purpose. But it's a small world.

That night, a couple of the fishermen from the boat were cleaning up in the shower room at the state park where they were staying, when they got laughing about what had taken place that day out on the lake. How funny it had been to watch the Game Warden going over the back of the boat into the drink, in slow motion ! They had a great time reliving the story to each other.

They never thought for a minute that in one of the other shower stalls was a trooper from the Manistique state police post. He was also staying at the state park. When this trooper heard the story and realized that the Game Warden had made all the fishermen swear they would never tell a soul about his misfortune, well you know the rest of what happened. Conservation Officers' follies for some reason are hard to keep a secret.

"Thanks"

For years up here in the U.P. there was a real problem with poachers going into the deer yards (this is where the deer go, usually a cedar swamp, to spend the winter when the snow gets deep) and shooting them illegally. For this reason, the Game Warden spent a lot of time working the deer yards and checking out vehicles driving back into them.

A good Game Warden has to be on the lookout for even the littlest things that may be out of a person's normal pattern. For example: There was the time that one of the locals, driving a logging truck with a high load of logs on it, passed a Game Warden in his patrol car. As the officer passed the truck, the driver never looked to the right or left but stared straight ahead. The driver never stopped, or even slowed down to acknowledge the Game Warden's presence on the 2-track logging road. After passing this truck on this narrow 2-track road, the officer started thinking, because this logger was one of those that always stopped and talked an arm and leg off the Conservation Officer whenever he saw him. The Game Warden turned around and went back to check the logging truck out. While looking around, he found three illegal deer that had been thrown up on top the load of logs. They had all been shot out of season. This officer always said that if the guy driving the logging truck had just stopped and talked with him like he always did, he would have never seen the deer hide up on top the load or even thought of checking him out.

Another time, a Game Warden was going to work back in a deer yard where there was a logging job going on. As he was going down a 2-track road, he met a pickup coming out. He stopped to talk to the people in the pickup, and as he stood there talking, he saw that there was snow and brush in the back of the truck. The Game Warden put his hand down in the snow in the back of the truck and felt a deer leg. Upon checking the truck out, he found the poachers had a couple of deer that they had killed illegally buried in the snow and brush in the back of the truck. The officer was definitely glad that his suspicions had led him to check things out.

A couple of weeks later, this same Game Warden was again working the same deer yard for poachers. This time, he came upon a much larger truck that was loaded with snow and even had a shovel stuck in the snow on the back of the truck. The officer put two and two together, came up with six, jumped out of his patrol car, talked to the guy by the truck, then jumped up on the back of the truck and started to shovel the snow off the back. The officer worked up quite a sweat because this was a good size truck and the snow was deep. When he got down so far that there could not be anything hidden under the snow, he put the shovel down, wiped the sweat away, and got down off the truck. The guy standing there, who had watched the whole thing without saying a word, now said, "Thanks a lot, John. I just pulled down here before you came to shovel all the snow that had built up off the back of my truck, and I sure appreciate the hand you gave me." Oh, well, things are not always what you hope they will be !

Watch Your Step:

Did you ever try something that should be so simple and - usually is under normal circumstances - but when you are in uniform, in front of people, things do not always turn out just like you had them planned. One real problem I always had when I was working (and I never figured out how to solve it) was getting into a canoe gracefully. I have, while out in the middle of nowhere all by myself, gotten in and out of canoes dozens of times without a problem, but let there be people around I am still perfecting the art involved in stepping into a canoe.

Here I stand, naturally there are a number of people around, with the canoe on the edge of a stream. All my gear has been loaded in the canoe, and I am ready to get going. Now remember, I am in full uniform, driving a marked patrol car, so there is no secret as to who and what I am. I put on my life vest and step to the water's edge. While holding onto the edge of the canoe to steady it, I put one foot into the canoe. I am still holding the canoe tight against the shore. Just as I go to step into the canoe with my other foot, while foot number one is still in the canoe,(number two foot is now up in the air) the canoe decides to move slowly away from the shore heading downstream ! It moves quite slowly, but still too fast to place foot number two back on the bank. I cannot let go of the canoe or the current will take it downstream with all my gear in it. I cannot jump into the canoe like I would a boat or the canoe will tip over. So, as gracefully as I can, I step into the water, up to my uniform pockets, with one foot (number one) still hung up in the canoe. Now, I am really in a bind. I have one leg waist deep in the water, the other foot is still in the canoe, and my hand is now between my legs hanging onto the edge of the canoe ! This is really quite a move for a 6'3", 230 pound guy to get himself into.

All this time, the people standing there are thinking about the strange way a Game Warden has of getting into a canoe. The only thing left to do is to pull foot number one out of the canoe and place it waist deep in the water next to foot number two, acting all the time like this was all part of my plan that I had laid out for the day before I ever left home.

Now, if you see a Game Warden driving an unmarked truck, going out on patrol wearing plain clothes, with a canoe on the back of his unmarked truck, he may be worth following, and you now know why. Because in an unmarked truck, in plain clothes if he falls into the drink he can act like a tourist, and nobody will ever know the difference.

Chapter 9

WINTER, GIRL'S WONDERLAND ?

As you well know, if you know anything about Michigan's U.P., we have snow the biggest part of the year, or so it seems. With all this snow, it is only natural that we do a lot of snowmobiling. This fact, as well as the job I have held for twenty-five years, puts me well over 30,000 miles on snow machines. Most of the trips were the type you really enjoyed, then returned home to file them in the back of your mind thinking, "Boy, it was a great day to be out there enjoying the beautiful U.P." But then every once in awhile you run into a trip that, no matter how hard you try, you cannot get it out of your mind. This was that type of trip, mind-boggling ! The kind when you do get home and pass out in your chair, you say, "Man, what a day !!"

We had the time of our lives last weekend, that is, if you want to take a few years off your life, see if you are in great physical shape, and quickly face the fact that you are not, or if you think you may be a little insane and want to go over the edge !!

Last weekend, there were about twenty girls from the Saginaw area that came up here to snowmobile. Now most of the girls had never ridden a snowmobile before, so it was their first trip, out. On this first trip I was lucky enough to get to go along. Well, they were riding 1960 snow machines in 1990, so what could go wrong? These machines were not high speed racing machines even back in 1960 when they were new. In fact, with the girls riding them they had little or no top speed at all. So again, what could go wrong ?

Our plans were to start out from the Ramada Inn here in Manistique, with these twenty girls and about fifteen snow machines. We were heading north about twenty miles to Ollie Rehn's cabin as a mid-trip point to have some hot chocolate, and then return to town. As I said, this cabin is only about twenty miles from town, located right off a groomed snowmobile trail. Ollie had gone up to the cabin to make the hot chocolate and warm it up while waiting for us to get there. It is just about a half hour ride from town to his cabin when running on the groomed trails under normal conditions. But !! We were soon to find out these definitely were not going to be normal conditions!

I have never in my forty years of riding snow machines gone anywhere so slowly ! Not even when our snow machines had six horsepower engines with wooden cleats on the tracks!   Believe it or not !!!

I would never have thought that so many girls could get so many snow machines stuck so often. We would have to stop, pull them out, point them to the trail, then start them out again. Finally, we got them out of the Ramada Inn parking lot. For some reason, we could not convince the girls that it is a lot easier to steer a snow machine if you give it enough gas to make the track at least go around than if you don't give it any gas. You have to at least try to go this fast ! We finally made it from the Ramada Inn to the other side of town (four blocks). In this amount of time a normal snowmobiler would have been up to Ollie's cabin drinking hot chocolate already. But the fun had only begun !

At this point, we left the west side of town. Now here you have to cross the dam at Intake park by the city waterworks system. Here you are crossing the Indian River on a bridge built on top of the dam for just snowmobiles (it is rather narrow). At this point we may have been better off to have placed a blindfold on the girls that were driving the snow machines rather than letting them see this bridge. We soon became well aware of this by the looks on their faces when they first saw this bridge. But things went pretty well, and only one machine missed the bridge.

We finally made it to the Haywire Snowmobile Trail and pointed our crew north toward the cabin. At this point we had our first fatality, our first snow machine died. It was one we had borrowed from a party in town, one of only three that we were responsible for. After one attempted pull on the starter rope, I knew from having been through it before, that CPR was not going to help this machine. I figure that 90% of all snowmobiles have air-cooled engines. For this reason, would it not be logical that in order to cool off the engine you have to move forward fast enough to cause the air to move around the engine in order to cool it off ? Could this have been our problem with the girls driving them ? Just Kidding..

Well, we doubled up and started off again. We are already almost two whole miles from town. At this point, on a nice straight snowmobile trail (an old railroad grade), I am riding right behind a girl on an old Snow-jet machine. She is moving along at the normal speed, for a girl, when she comes to an old railroad bridge that she is supposed to cross. Only she didn't !! Well, she did make it halfway across this bridge. Then, she must have finally figured out how to turn a snowmobile. She turned hard to the left and drove right off the side of the bridge !! It is "only" about a six to eight foot drop to the ice below, also a heart attack for the adult riding on the machine behind her. We got her out and back on the trail, and she was unhurt. You have to remember the speed she was traveling at when she went over the edge. But it took us a whole lot of sweat, plus going through the ice, to get the girl's machine back on the trail. We also had to add this machine to our fatality list, for as we pointed the machine north to continue the trip, the skis wanted to go to the west. Two snow machines down already ! Double up again, then off we go again. Besides, this girl did not want to be a driver anymore anyway.

In the next eight miles, between the S-curves and M-94 at the Jackpine lodge, snow machines three and four went to the Happy Hunting Grounds. This makes four of our machines now parked along the side of the trail. Now plans had to be re-made seeing this was supposed to be a twenty mile trip one way. By now, we had only gone about twelve miles, plus the afternoon was about gone. We are a good two hours behind in our plans to stop at Ollie's cabin. Using the best part of our minds that were left, the leaders decided to turn the whole crew of girls around and head back towards the Ramada Inn ! Great !! Back toward town. We did send someone to Ollie's cabin to break the news to him, "The five gallons of hot chocolate are all yours !" Besides it would either be ruined or spoiled by the time we got there.

We made it all the way back to the Ramada Inn with only two near misses, also, one girl trying to move an immovable object. Crews of men were then sent out to recover the downed snow machines we had left along the trails.

After supper, the girls decided they were ready to go again. The only thing was, the leader of the leaders had to threaten the other leaders with their lives to find anyone who wanted to go out with a crew of girls for another snowmobile trip.

Chapter 10

HAPPY HUNTERS

When you spend the biggest part of your life riding around checking on and talking to hunters and fishermen, you run into some things that just make you want to laugh. Now to get the proper feeling for these tales you have to put yourself in the right frame of mind to be at the time and place where these stories took place.

One day, I was on patrol a good forty miles from the nearest town. There was a new snow on the ground that made it nice for the Game Warden who wanted to check up on hunters that normally walk way back into the middle of nowhere just so they will not be checked. At least this is what goes through the Game Warden's mind. Now you have to remember that most hunters hunt within twenty-five feet of a road. So, if they get lost they can always see the headlights of the cars on the road after it gets dark. If any officer worth his salt finds a set of tracks that lead him back across hill and dale, the more he walks, the more his mind starts to work. Pretty soon all the officer can think about is the fact that no hunter in his right mind would walk this far back in, unless, he was doing something that he did not want anybody to know he was doing especially the Game Warden !

On this day, while out on patrol during the firearm deer season, I saw a set of tracks in the new snow going off through the marsh. I parked my truck and took off following these tracks over ridge after ridge, through the low marshes... I walked and walked back to the middle of that spot called "the middle of nowhere" and about a mile beyond. Here I found a party that had shortly before I arrived shot a really nice eight pointbuck. This big buck would easily weigh, well over 200 pounds. This hunter was as happy as could be. Even when I told him that the only way he was ever going to get his deer out was to air-lift it, it did not seem to bother him.

This hunter told me that he had been hunting deer for eight years, and this was his first buck. He had paid $100.00 for his license plus his wife had bought him a new deer rifle for this trip. It seems it was a gift from her on the birth of their baby boy who had just arrived before deer season. I told him he could leave the deer and go get some help to drag it out. NO WAY !! He was from the "city" and was worried that someone would come along and steal it while he was gone. I told him, "Man, they could never find it to steal it ! Besides, there are a lot of deer a lot closer to a road to steal before you would want to go through all the work to steal this one !" I also told him that the only two human beings within miles of this place were the two of us. He was not about to leave his deer.

This hunter had on a full snowmobile suit, a good wool shirt, heavy wool coveralls, a shirt, a sweater, and all of his regular clothes. He also had his gun and a 35MM camera outfit with him. I asked him where his hunting buddies were. He told me that they had all headed for home the day before. He was up here hunting all alone now.

He had just cleaned his deer and asked me if I knew where the gallbladder was on a deer. I then looked down at his deer's gut pile and saw where he had laid out all the insides like he was doing an autopsy ! He wanted to know what his deer had been eating, how healthy it was. and I guess what made it tick. Here I was standing saying to myself, "Do you know how far you have to drag this thing? !! You're going to wish it was a spike horn before you even get it to a road. " But he was in his glory, and nobody was going to tell him any different. He told me, " I'll drag it a little ways and rest, then drag it a little more. I have all day to get it out to my truck." As I turned to go on my way, he just asked, "Check back about midnight; if my truck is still parked out there, send some help." I checked for his truck at midnight, and he was out and gone.

THE TRACKER:

I left the area above and drove down the road a little way. I got near the Steuben area on a 2-track road. I saw this hunter standing back in the woods on the side of a hill, so I stopped and went back to talk with him. It turned out to be a gal. As I walked up, I saw her tracks and those of a real large deer. I asked her if I could check her hunting license. She got this funny look on her face and said, " Oh No ! I went back to the cabin to put some lipstick on and left it on the table." I cannot figure out for the life of me why you would have to wear lipstick to hunt "Deer".??

I asked how she was doing, and she told me, "There is a rally big buck here, and I saw it yesterday !" She also stated, "I can tell these are its tracks, and it's really big for it has these large points on the back of its tracks ! My husband told me that's how you tell it's a really big buck."

She then informed me that she had returned today to get back on its track, which she was now following. She was going to track it down. I had noticed one thing about her tracks and that of the deer when I first walked up to her. She was back-tracking the deer ! The large points that were "on the back of the track" were really the points on the front of a deer's track. She was going East and the deer had gone West. Off she went after her big buck, happy as could be. I did not have the heart to ruin her day by telling her the news. Besides, I hear that deer have been known to make big circles in their travels at times, so who knows...just maybe.

Chapter 11

Deer Season:

For just about all my life, or at least for as long as I can remember, I have been going to hunting camps. Also, my job for the past twenty-five years has been as a game warden checking hunters. For this reason, you come across a lot of stories about what happens while people are out hunting. I guess the strange things you hear about never end.

The stories are heard as one hunter tells on another. Some I know are 100% true, while others may be a little dressed up by the teller to just rib his buddy a little. Some are mine, while some were told to me by others.

One On The Game Warden:

In order to be a successful game warden, your mind has to be working all the time. You have to look for the little things that put you on the right track so you can catch a poacher; sometimes maybe you look to hard.

Now there was this game warden that was a throwback to the old school. He would hear of some illegal activity and get right out there to work on it. After this officer had received information about some illegal deer hunting, he took a ride to the area. When he arrived at the deer yard, (besides seeing a lot of deer) he observed a vehicle. He parked to check this other vehicle out. It had not been there long, for the engine was still hot. It was getting toward evening when the deer should be moving, which made this a good bet. If the outlaws were back in the woods, he would get where he could watch their truck. Now all he had to do was wait them out.

He found his spot, and now he was all set. His patrol vehicle was out of sight, but not their vehicle. (In the vast areas that you patrol up here in the U.P., you may be a long walk from any town. You also have to have the patience of "Job" to wait the poachers out. You don't want to get tired of sitting, and as a result, move too quickly) The officer waited, and time went by.

One hour, he figured they must be back in there up to no good. Two hours, this is looking better all the time. Three hours, another supper missed. It is now getting dark. They must be waiting until after dark to bring the deer out.

All of a sudden he sees someone around the vehicle with a flashlight. Now headlights! He starts the patrol car and flies down the road to where the truck is parked. The moment of truth!! Now he has them cold! The long wait was worth it. Wait! Wait! There is another vehicle there! He pulls up and finds one of the local wreckers hooking onto the truck, the one he had been watching for over three hours. He walks over to the wrecker and finds out that the truck had broken down. The owner then had to walk all the way back to town and send a wrecker out. The officer had sat and waited for almost four hours! Another cold supper when he gets home. The worst part, "It was all for nothing." But it had looked so promising.

HOT LIPS:

Up here in the U.P. during early bow season, we may get cold snowy weather. Also, a lot of the 2-track roads on private land have cables across them to keep unwanted people out. For this reason, a hunter has to be ready for everything. Now, there was this bow hunter that was going up to some private land to hunt on a ridge. It had been a cold week with rain and snow. He pulled up to the cable across the 2-track and got out with his key to unlock it. As he tried to get his key in the lock, he found out the lock was frozen. He bent over, trying to blow into the key slot to get the ice out. He could not get the ice out of the slot, and the key still would not go in. He got his mouth right up against the padlock, but here he made a startling discovery! His lips were now firmly attached to the padlock, which was firmly attached to the cable, which was firmly hooked around two trees. He was in real trouble!! There was no way he could get his lips off the padlock.

Now he couldn't get back to his truck. He couldn't get to his blind. He could not go anywhere, as long as he was part of this padlock. The best way to get loose would be to somehow heat the padlock up to the temperature of his lips. Then, they would release themselves from the padlock. But hooked up this way, how could he do it. There was only one way.

He took a deep breath, gritted his teeth, and then jerked his lips off the padlock!! (Leaving half of them still attached). Then, he spent the next two weeks at work explaining what in the world happened to his lips!!

Things have to get better, right? Up here in this country, we have a fifteen day firearm deer season in the middle of bow season, so our friend does not have to worry about going through the cable back to his bow blind. He is all set up with a rifle blind. He plans to spend some time trying to get a deer this way.

One day, he is sitting out in his blind. Things are kind of slow. To kill time, he decides to practice taking the safety on his firearm on and off, in order to see how quietly he can make it work. This can be a trick. If you have ever hunted from a blind, you know that the metal click when you switch a safety to the fire position on a rifle can scare a deer off. So here he sits, practicing how quietly he can take the safety off. He only had one problem. To be safe, he has pointed the firearm up in the air, but the butt plate has come to rest where in just a few seconds he is going to wish it had not, barrel up, but plate down. You see, as he played with his safety, his finger must have hit the trigger causing his 30.06 to go off. As he lay there turning thirty-seven different shades of green, he realized that it is really important to make sure where both ends of a firearm are pointing.

The old "Game Wardens" crew

John Walker

Illegal ducks taken out of season.

Big buck (cover) shot out of season.

Illegal fish from Thompson Creek

*Working on
Ilegal deer
shooting in
deer yard
party was
caught with
aid of these
tire tracks.*

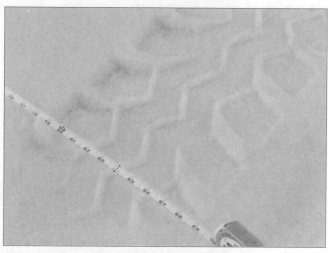

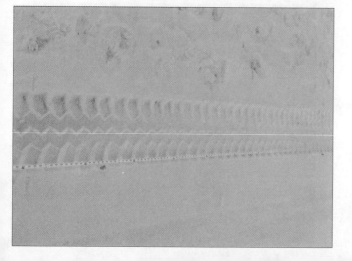

Fawn head and hide found in green trash box.

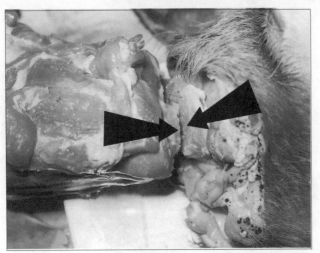

State police crime lab matched roast from freezer to fawn neck from trash. Jury found party guilty.

Seized from freezer in stores.

Illegal gill nets with fish in them.

Trunk with 70 Illegal Walleye.

Illegal Walleye.

The new Deer Camp.

Along with the old.

My boys at Deer Camp.

Dad, Me, and my sister 1947.

Dad with grandson at camp.

Dad and boys.

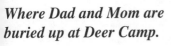

*Where Dad and Mom are
buried up at Deer Camp.*

The old snowmobiles (bought in 1960).

U.P. Boys on a Saturday before TV.

HELP ME PLEASE:

Now to get the true feeling for this story, you have to picture a few facts. Back twenty-five years ago, the main job of a game warden was to catch poachers. For this reason, we seldom wore uniforms during deer season. Since we drove around in unmarked trucks, we could not be picked out quite as easily.

On this early morning patrol, my partner and I were in plain clothes, and we were driving an old beat-up International pickup. We came to a 2-track trail through state land. We decided to take it. As we came down the trail, there was a red pine plantation. It was right in front of us, off to the left side of the road. Just as we were going by, a hunter stepped out onto the trail. It surprised us for a minute. Now, as a game warden, you soon learn to tell a real hunter from a dude. You know, someone that tries to act like he belongs in the woods, but does not fit. For this reason, we stopped. He came to the truck, and I asked him, "How are you doing?" He looked at me for a minute, then said, "I can't really tell." Now this was a dumb answer to my question. It did not fit. So I asked him, "What do you mean?" He stated, "I can't find its horns." Wow! This really did not fit. So very carefully, I reached down to shut off the radio, so nobody would call us before we got to the bottom of this.

I got out of the truck and told him we would help him find the horns. He agreed, so we went off walking through the pine plantation. As we came to the other side, I saw a deer lying there. Right away I could tell it was a big doe. I walked up. looked at it, and said, "I can't find any horns either." He said, "It's a doe, ain't it?" I told him it was. "What do I do now?" I told him that he did not have to do a thing, for we were already here. We then told him we were game wardens.

Maybe Next Year:

I was talking to this young guy that really has a great time hunting. His success is about zero, but he does like to hunt. He was telling me about all the deer he missed one year. First, there was bow season where he missed his share and someone else's, too. Then rifle season came along. He figured his chances would get better, since they couldn't get much worse.

This young lad hunts on his uncle's pig farm in Northern Wisconsin. In Wisconsin, a firearm deer hunter can hunt from a tree stand. With the open area of the farm and the number of deer around, how could he miss? I don't know, but he did. It seems that the first couple of days he figured he missed about half-dozen deer. I asked him if he ever sighted his rifle in, and he told me he did each year, but, it seems he had trouble hitting a target, too. Well, what could I say? I told him, "The law of average has to be on your side. If you shoot at enough deer, there has to be one that someday will run into a bullet."

A couple days later, he figured the law of averages had finally kicked in. He was up in his tree stand when this nice buck came across the field from his left. He waited until just the right minute to pull up and shoot. Down the buck went! Finally, he had scored. He got a deer! As he climbed down from the tree stand, he saw the buck lying on the ground twitching. He hit the ground to run over and check out the first deer he had ever gotten. Man! It was a buck! Just about the time he got to the deer, it jumped up and ran away! He was so surprised that he did not even shoot at it. How could this be?

He went over the where the deer had fallen down only to find that it had not fallen from his shot at all. It seems that his uncle had an electric fence to keep the pigs in. This fence was located about a foot off the ground, right through the field where his buck had run. As luck would have it, the buck tripped over the electric fence just as he shot. The buck then lay there twitching from the electric current (or laughing), not from being shot. Sometimes things just are just not what they appear to be at first. Well, there's always next year.

Chapter 12

HUNTING WIFEE

Up in this country, during the fall of the year, there is only one thing to do, enjoy the outdoors, and guys usually take advantage of it. For this reason, most men from this neck of the woods hunt from the start of the first hunting season, September 10th, until the end of rabbit season, March 31st. When a guy has this problem, if the wifee wants to see her husband, to talk to him, she has to take up hunting. (They get to talk between stops and to and from their deer blinds.) There are more and more wives all the time taking up hunting with their husbands. Here are a couple of stories about hunting wifees.

Wifee's Opening Morning:

There was this hunter that was informed by his wife that she would like to go deer hunting with him. So, he went out before season and looked his hunting area over to find a nice spot to build a blind for her to hunt from. He fixed up a nice deer blind for his dear, and when it was done, it had all the comforts of home, almost. It is nothing up in the U.P. to have a good part of the firearm deer season with below-zero weather. For this reason, a lot of the deer blinds are enclosed to protect the hunter from the cold weather and snow. The man had built the blind and baited the deer runway that ran right in front of it. Things looked good, and everything was all set.

Now his blind was right over the ridge just a short distance from where the wife would be sitting. If anything came up he would be right there, but yet he had his own area and his deer runway to worry about. Opening day right at daybreak had always been one of the best times for him, and there were both rubs and scrapes near his blind. Things looked prime.

When opening morning came, they got up well before daylight to get ready. The plans were to get into their deer blinds a good hour before daylight, then just sit and let things settle down before the first light of dawn. A lot of times, right at dawn, a buck will be on the move looking for does and walk right into a baited area. Well, the couple set out. First the husband stopped at the wife's blind to drop her off. He dumped a little bait, made sure her heater was going and she was all set, now just sit quietly and wait. Now you want to get into these blinds without making any noise and do as little moving around as possible. If you are an avid hunter, you have this all down to a science so you will not spook the deer. Wifee is all set up in her blind well before daylight. She is instructed to just sit nice and still, make no noise, just wait for dawn to break, and just maybe...

Her husband is now off running to get to his blind. He gets all set up in his, and there is still enough time for things to settle down. Things seemed to have worked out pretty good timing wise. Now here he sits, half asleep, dreaming of about forty-five minutes from now when the big one will walk in. (They always do in your dreams.) Dawn is now just around the corner. Judgment time is here. Was all his work going to pay off? Relax, wait, when all of a sudden there is this scream that vibrates through the whole woods !!!! He about jumps through the roof of his blind. When the shock wears off, he realizes it came from over the other side of the ridge, right where his wifee's blind is ! He is tempted to stay seated, because it is just about time for deer to start moving. (If they have not all been killed by the shock of that death curdling scream a few minutes ago).

But, since that blood-curdling scream had come from his wifee's deer blind, off he goes, running over the ridge and through the woods to her blind. He gets there only to find that his wifee is a basket case.

It seems that all was going along just like it was supposed to. She was in her blind being nice and still and quiet. It was still dark, all was quiet around her,and dawn was just a short time away. All of a sudden, she felt something move down by her foot. About this same time, her hand dropped down to feel what it was; she felt hair !!! Out came that blood-curdling scream. It was just a reflex reaction ! Looking down she could just make out the shape of a skunk. It seems that it had moved into her blind to live. What a deal, a nice warm blind with a nice warm object to curl up against before going to sleep. Opening morning or not! Having been told by her husband to keep quiet or not! The scream just came out when her hand made contact with hair where there shouldn't have been any hair.

From Work To Blind, Non-Stop:

Up here in the U.P., hunting is the highlight of a man's life. The only problem is that there is one thing that always seems to come up and interfere with a guy's hunting. WORK ! So you have to plan around this problem, because its a necessary evil, and you just have to learn to live with it.

The way you handle this is to get off day shift, make a run for home in record time, grab all your gear, and run for your hunting spot. All this takes expert planning and timing to make it work. If you have hunted deer with a bow, you know that this has become a high-tech sport. The bows in use now are walking computers. Plus, when you find a perfect hunting spot, it seems that all the small deer have moved in close to your home, and the biggest and nicest bucks are twenty or thirty miles away, one way. You do find just the right spot, put up your tree stand, set out your bait, then return home and get all your gear together.

You need just the right gear to blend into the tree you hunt from. You also need to have a mask or paint your face so the deer won't know who shot at it. That way its family cannot get revenge on your garden next spring. You have set everything up, planned out everything to a tee and are all set. Check: You need your boots, hat, scent bags, gloves, coffee, lunch, bait, knife, rope, deer tag, string to tie it on, and bait bucket, also a cushion to sit on and a camera-just in case. You are all set with this along with your flashlight, tracking string, tracking ribbon, a plastic bag to put the deer heart in, and fresh bait.

Your at work, but now your shift is over. Out the door, off you go across the parking lot for your truck. You fly home, run in, drop your clothes as you go, into your hunting clothes, and grab: your camo-suit, lunch, coffee, scent bags, gloves, boots, face paint, flashlight, heater seater, knife, hat, mask, bait and bucket, rope, and make sure you have your kill tag ! Off to the truck, you are on your way. Right on schedule, in record time ! You are cutting it close, but things look good. You drive the thirty miles to your hunting spot. You jump out as you finish your coffee, paint your face, eat your sandwich that tastes like paint, put on your warm boots, camo-suit, (better do now what you can't do from your tree stand because of all the coffee you drank), mask, hat, gloves, flashlight, knife, etc. Bait goes into the bucket and we are about ready !! Grab your bow and off..bow..bow.. thirty miles from home, you have everything you need, but your bow and arrows ! Anything else you could, maybe get along without, but not your bow and arrows ! This is the one item it is suggested that you not forget ! But the worse part is yet to come !

Throw stuff back into the truck, and off you go the thirty miles, all the way back home. You come spinning into the drive with gravel flying; you jump out and tear through the door ! Wifee is standing there with your bow in her hand saying, "Get anything, honey ?"

Don't you think that wifee should have helped pack all your hunting gear so you would have had someone to blame when you forgot your bow ?

P.S. These stories are true. You would be amazed how many hunters get out in the woods and find they forgot their firearm, bow, or some other items you cannot hunt without, shells or arrows for instance.

Chapter 13

THE OLD FASHIONED WAY

Well, I have told a number of stories during the last couple of years, like the one about us boys trapping. A lot of these stories were about growing up over in the Ontonagon area of the U.P. I think about my stories like these, when I watch a TV program like the one I saw the other night. This show talked about the problems parents are having with their kids in this day and age. They talked about the how's and why's of raising kids, and what parents should do today. It seems that so many kids have no goals in their life. They just want to drink, party, and have "fun" all the time.

It's funny, but I know the answer to the problems that they were talking about, that parents face with today's youth. Just think, I know all this without their college education !

The answer to their problem is to let every kid have a Mom and Dad like I did. Now there were six kids in our tribe, and we were not angels by a long shot. Maybe the girls were, but girls are strange.

One Saturday morning, I got a call from my brother who lives near Green Bay, Wisconsin, saying that Mom had gone to be with our Dad who had passed away over twenty years ago. We have all gone through a time when someone super special dies. We sit and think about all the good times that were had. Believe it or not, I cannot recall a bad time with my parents. Now let me tell you, in today's language, I was what you would call an abused child ! I got some real lickings with the old razor strap ! Those guys that will tell you that a spanking with a razor strap does not hurt never had my Dad dishing it out from the other end for all he was worth. I got whip 'uns ! Where in this day and age, they would call out the troops from the U.N. to protect me. The thing is, even back then, I knew I had earned them.

There is one thing I knew through all those times, and that is that my Mom and Dad loved me. You would have had to be there to see Mom, she got into hunting clothes that were way too big, so her boy could go out hunting. You see, in Michigan, you have to be seventeen to hunt alone. Since Dad would be working afternoon shift at the paper mill, in order for me to get to go hunting Mom would get bundled up in hunting gear and go sit with me. Now my Mom never hunted. But she knew her boy really liked to, so off we would go, out on a deer runway, so she could sit and freeze. Never a complaint and never saying, "See all I do for you !" She was just Mom, and I needed an adult to go with me. So, off she went.

Then, there were the years that the paper mill was shut own. Mom and all of us kids picked night-crawlers all night long, to help pay for things when the bills were due. Since we only got twenty-five cents a dozen, we had to pick a lot of them. We always did things together, we were a family. Us kids never went without even when we made our money this way, because Mom and dad made it work.

I can still remember the times we would go up to clean out deer camp. Just before the start of firearm deer season. I knew if you got into camp first, to look inside the old wood cook stove, in here you would find a nest of deer mice (Out in a field they are called field mice, but inside a deer camp they are called deer mice). We would catch them and place them in a quart jar to take home for pets. (Now they sell them at pet stores, or at least they look the same.) We would walk into the house, as proud as could be with our catch, Mom would just shake her head and give Dad one of "those" looks. I sit here and remember that my Dad always took his vacation the first week of deer season. Dad would spend it at deer camp with his brother and cousins from down state, who he only saw once a year. But Dad always managed to get back to town a couple of times during season. He would pick up the boys to let them spend a couple of nights at deer camp with the men. There was always time for us in his plans.

One time, we kids asked Mom, "How come we never take a vacation like other families do ?" Dad always used his one week a year vacation during deer season, that was all you got back in those days. Mom told us kids, "Dad spends all year long working at the paper mill, so we can have a nice warm home and food to eat. Now, this week belongs to him, to spend with his brothers." There was never a bitter feeling from anyone. I can remember only two real vacations in all the time I lived at home.

I also remember how mad us boys would get when Dad would not shoot at a nice buck, because he hoped it would walk by one of us boys. It was a bigger thrill for Dad if one of us got a chance at a deer, then if he got one. Dad always wanted us to have a good time. He was just the way a Dad was suppose to be.

I can sit here and hear Mom right now, My mom used to say, if Dad started the car, loaded up the family, and never touched the steering wheel, it would go up the Norwich Road to hunting camp all by itself !" (Dad was born up there, where the old homestead was.) You see, this was where we always went as a family to do things, to spend time together. Now, out of this tribe of Walkers, we have an engineer, a police chief, a school teacher, an accountant, and a Conservation Officer. We played together, had fun together, and we now miss Mom together.

That year after the frost was out of the ground, we took one last trip up to the old deer camp with Mom. Up the Norwich Road, to the Walkerville Camp. We went across the field to the area under the big Oak tree. See, this is where my Dad had waited over twenty years for my Mom.

You see, my youngest brother, Tim, he is mentally retarded. Dad and Tim always spent time up at hunting camp together. Dad always told him, "Tim, someday Mom and I are going to come up to camp and stay. We'll be over under the big Oak tree. You'll not be able to see us Tim, but we'll be here every time you get to come up to deer camp." Now they are, where they always wanted to be together.

You ask me how to raise kids today ? I'll tell you, do it the same way my Mom and Dad did it, love them, correct them, do things with them, and make them something special in your life.

P.S. You have one of the best natural tools to use up here, Michigan's great outdoors, the good old U.P.

Chapter 14

A DEER GETS REVENGE

(Standing Tall)

When I first moved into Schoolcraft county in the Michigan U.P., it was the mid-70's. The favorite team sport in the county, at that time, was illegally shining for deer at night with a spotlight. In this area it had been handed down through the ages. Some of the clans were famous for their activities in this sport. On a dull night, they would pick up a 12-pack, a spotlight, and a gun, to go out to spot light for deer. Back then if you did get caught, it only cost you about twenty bucks. So what cheaper way to have a good nights fun ? While maybe even getting some meat to eat too boot. This story is one of those about a crew that gets caught out hunting deer at night with a spot light. Now remember, this is Michigan's U.P. and these brothers for years have been telling their Game Warden stories in the bars around Schoolcraft county.

It was a nice clear fall evening when the local forest fire officer and myself went to work. We were going to work the area around Port Inland quarry. (The very Southeastern corner of the county) In this area there is not a house for miles in any direction, but there are a lot of deer. Back then, as I have stated before, we would spend hours driving around after dark without any headlights on. This night, after dark, we were going down a two-track road in the Southeast corner of Schoolcraft county where it goes into Mackinac county. We had our windows down, our headlights out, and we were only going a few miles an hour. All of a sudden the fire officer whispered that he had just heard a gunshot! Close! I stopped to wait, shutting off the car. A few seconds later there was a second shot fired. We started the car, pulled forward a couple hundred yards, and stopped to block the road. Thereby blocking the only way out of the area from which we heard the shot. We then waited.

A little while later, a pickup truck came toward us. We stopped it using only our flashlights and found one person in it. While checking the truck, we found some 22-rifle shells. While checking the truck, the driver told us he was just out riding round for the evening by himself. We did not believe him, but he was let go on his way.

I went down to the next corner, still without headlights. The fire officer jumped out of the patrol vehicle, with a hand held radio, to hide in the ditch. The only slight problem we had was it's hard to tell just how fast you are going in the dark without your headlights on. Then do you know what happens to a Fire Officer's body stepping out of a patrol car going 10-15 miles-per-hour in the dark on a gravel road ? But all is well that ends well, He lived. We knew there had to be more then the one person from the pickup in the area. I went down another two-track road to hide the patrol car, here I waited until the fire officer called me. He said that he had two fellows stopped on the road where I had left him. I went out and found him with two of the most famous "deer hunters" from the county. (This is according to bar talk) I talked to them and they stated that they were just out for a walk (15 miles from the closest house). One had a hand- held, sealed-beam flashlight. When I looked at the flashlight, I saw it had spots of fresh blood on it !

When I asked them about what looked to be fresh blood, I was told it was coyote blood from earlier that day (it was still wet). Now just a few month before I moved up here, the Michigan State Police had placed a crime lab in the U.P. for the first time. Before this it was 300 miles to the nearest crime lab to get any work done on our cases. For this reason, most of these local boys had never dealt with a crime lab expert going over the evidence. For years they had been able to tell the local Game Warden it was "Coyote Blood" and gotten away with it because the officer could not prove different, because if we could not prove them wrong, they won. But now we could drive the ninety miles to the U.P. crime lab and have work done on our cases. I did this, and it proved to be deer blood, but I'm getting ahead of the story. We got some information from the two brothers, then they headed down the same road the guy that had been out for a ride in his pickup, all by himself, had taken. We also knew that the driver of the pickup we had stopped earlier was a cousin of the two brothers, and that they ran around together. Now we have these two "famous" brothers walking down a road in the middle of the night, miles from home, without a vehicle, needless to say, we did not believe them either.

The fire officer and myself went up the road the way the two brothers had come from to look around. In the dew on the ground, we could see where someone had moved around out in an opening in the trees. We could follow the tracks across the opening, then back in the direction of a Red Pine plantation. When we got out of the dew into the plantation, we would lose their tracks. We decided to spend the night sleeping in the Red Pine plantation to stay in the area where we felt there was evidence of illegal deer hunting. When daylight came, we picked up their tracks in the plantation. In a dead furrow, where the trees had been planted, we found a yearling deer that had been shot. We looked the whole area over real good. Later, we came across a 22-rifle with a scope hid in another dead furrow. Now we had a gun, a deer, plus the flashlight with blood on it from the two men.

We loaded the items in the patrol car and headed back to town. I stopped in town at the State Police Post for gas, and we told them what we had. To our surprise, we picked up another piece of evidence here at the post. It seems that the State Trooper that was working lived across the road from one of our two "famous" deer hunting brothers. The trooper told us that just before dark the night before, the brothers whom we had found walking down the road were sighting in a 22-rifle next to their garage, interesting.

Now we have all this evidence:

The deer, the gun (a 22-rifle), the troopers seeing the brothers sighting in a 22-rifle, plus the flashlight with blood on it, that was proven to be deer blood. BUT !!

You have to remember that up here in Michigan's U.P., back then, this did not always mean you could convict the party, you had caught for the illegal hunting he was involved in. In fact, it was so hard to get a conviction, that a lawyer from the big city down the road had a standing offer, if he lost a deer case in Schoolcraft county, he would buy the county prosecutor dinner. But at least, we would have our day in court with a jury trial.

Well, the day of the trial came. The jury was picked and there were a number of women on it. We felt it was a good jury, for this area. The case was going along with our side introducing the evidence. I was on the witness stand. We had placed the gun, the flashlight, and the shells from the pickup into evidence. Now we came to the deer. I was asked if we still had it, and I told them we did. We had kept it in the big walk-in freezer at the Thompson State Fish Hatchery, but it was now out in my car. I was told to go get the yearling deer we had found shot.

Now you have to picture this, you see Game Wardens have their sense of humor also. We had taken this little yearling fawn out to the Thompson

Fish Hatchery freezer, and froze it standing up !! Now I go out to my vehicle, to get this deer that is to be introduced as evidence against the defendant, as the jury sits in the courtroom and waits. I walk back into the courtroom carrying the deer under my arm. I walk down in front of the jury booth and the Judges bench and stop, then set our deer down standing up on its legs facing the jury. Now here is the victim, standing looking at the women on the jury with its big brown eyes, ears hanging down along the side its head. There is still grass in its mouth that it had been eating when it had been shot. When seeing this, the defendants' lawyer jumps to his feet, stating that they would stipulate that this was the deer in question, but he saw no need for it to stay in the courtroom. The Judge ruled in the deers favor and allowed it to remain standing there.

The case progressed into the afternoon. During mid-afternoon, the Judge gave the jury its instructions. When this was done the jury got ready to leave the courtroom to go into the jury room, to decide the verdict in the case. As they were walking out, the deer must have gotten tired of standing all day, or "Things" were just on our side, for the deer fell over and laid down almost at the juries feet. It seems the heat from the courtroom had thawed the deer out just enough to let it take the final bow ! The party was quickly found guilty and the big city lawyer has not been back, even to buy dinner.

By the way, today, almost twenty years later, I will see these two "famous" (they really were after this case) brothers at coffee. They will still give me a hard time about how unfair it was to use our star performer against them like we did. I tell them if they had not been such a bad shot, therefore having to fire the second shot, we maybe would never have caught them.

They also try to convince me that they turned over a new leaf after that night and gave up night hunting. Who knows, maybe they did, I never caught them again.

Chapter 15

SCHOOLCRAFT COUNTY

(Michigan's U.P.)

I thought I would take a few minutes to tell you about the area I worked as a Michigan Game Warden, and the county I lived in. To make a circle of my area of responsibility, you could drive between 200 and 300 miles. It ran, on the West boundary, from the Garden peninsula on Big Bay De Noc in lake Michigan to Grand Marais on Lake Superior in Alger County. Along lake Superior through Luce County, to Whitefish Point in Chippewa County. Then, down the East side to the area of the Black River, in Mackinac County, now at Lake Michigan again. Then you would have the seventy miles back along the shores of Lake Michigan, to the Manistique area.

Now, for there to be five or six thousand people living in some of these counties year around, would be stretching it. There is a lot of "Nothing Land" that makes up a good portion of some of these counties.

I had to do some checking one time for a report, I checked and came up with the following information: In Schoolcraft County there 340 Inland lakes; these cover an area of 20,861 acres; there is, also, 734 miles of rivers, streams and their tributaries. This puts Schoolcraft County in Michigan's top ten for rivers and streams. There are a good many miles of these rivers and streams that are designated as Trout streams, of these streams and rivers, there are fifteen that run into Lake Michigan. This allows for steelhead, salmon and smelt runs up these streams on their spawning runs out of Lake Michigan. Within the area of Schoolcraft County there are 286,300 acres of state forest lands, and 122,462 acres of Federal Forest lands. There are, also, large holdings of corporation timber lands. All this land is open for public hunting and fishing. It was stated in this report, back in the 80's, that there is over twenty million dollars spent in Schoolcraft County each year by tourists.

You want to remember that the above statistics were just for Schoolcraft County, not for the areas in the other four counties that we worked out of our base in Manistique. For this reason, you always hear this remark, "I have hunted or fished all my life, but I have never been checked by a Game Warden." This should not be a surprise, but I wonder how many have been watched by the Game Warden and never knew it ?

GASLIGHTS:

One night, a Federal Wildlife Officer and I were out looking for illegal pike spearers. We had looked around and found a stream with a number of nice pike (lots of bait) in a deep hole under a bridge. It made for a great place for officers to hide. Where the bridge crossed the stream, we found that you could crawl up under the bridge near an abutment. You had a clear view of the stream, both ways, Plus all the time you were hidden from anyones view who was in the stream. It worked almost like a cave, and besides, you were only a little way from the hole with the fish in it.

We took to our hiding spot under the bridge, overlooking the pike, to wait. Suckers were legal to spear in this stream at this time, but the Northern Pike that were spawning here were protected.

We were sitting up there, under the bridge, in the dark, when a crew of fish spearers came down the stream. They had a couple of gas lanterns, so we could watch them for quite a ways. The lanterns also light up an area of the stream from bank to bank. It appeared they had been at it for a while and had consumed a few beers in their journey, they were loud and really carrying on. They stopped at the big hole right below our hiding spot to look for fish. While they were there, they got into an argument about getting checked by a Game Warden while out fishing. There was a great big guy standing there with a gas lantern, making a point of impressing all his buddies as to what he would tell and do, if a Game Warden ever stopped to check him out. He told, how he would tell the Game Warden off the minute he was ask if he had a fishing license ! He was pretty blunt in what he was saying and was really impressive.

We sat, not twenty feet, behind this guy and heard him tell his buddies all his tough talk about us. He was feeling pretty good and proud of the way his drinking buddies were impressed. All this time he was talking, a couple of the crew had checked out the hole for fish. They had observed the pike but made no attempt to spear them, so it was plain to see they were just after suckers. Finally, one more time, Loud Mouth, the big guy holding the light, repeated, "You can bet your bottom dollar I'd never show a Game Warden a fishing license, if he ever asked me for one !!"

From under the hollow part of the bridge, not over twenty feet behind Mr. Tough Guy, came the Federal Officers deep voice saying,"Wanna

Bet!!" You see, this guy and his buddies had been under this bridge for about a half-hour thinking they were all alone with only them and the great unknown out there. All this time telling his buddies his opinion of things and never really planning on ever having to answer for what he said. He thought they were the only human beings for miles around. All of a sudden! this voice of doom comes out from under the bridge, in the dark right behind him, with a hollow sound made from the echo from the hole back under the abutment.

It really is amazing how far a big guy can throw a Colman gas lantern, when he is scared half out of his wits by a voice from out of the dark.

FLYING LEAP:

One other time we were working along this stream that had really high banks. Along the edge of this stream, between the water and the high banks, there had been so much traffic over the years there was a foot path. You could walk along the path with a gas light while looking for fish in the stream. Usually there would be a couple spearers in the water working their way upstream, while the gas lights were held to iluminate the water. We were working on a real bright moonlight night. This made it real easy for the Game Warden to walk all over without the aid of any flashlight. We just moved around in complete darkness. As usual, we were walking along the top of the high bank watching this crew down in the stream looking for fish. We observed this crew of four or five people coming along with their gas lights, we had a good view of them and they had no idea we were anywhere around. This time two were in the stream with spears and the gas lights and some were walking along the foot path watching them.

At this time of night, where they were, they thought they were the only ones in the area. There were no houses for miles and no sign of other people. As they worked their way by our vantage point, I slid down the bank and joined the three that were walking along the foot path on the edge of the stream. Where there had been three in a row, there were now four in a row walking along in the glow from their gas lights. (The last being about 230 pounds in a dark uniform)

From here I could see that the two in the stream were after suckers only, the season for spearing them was open.

All of a sudden ! a girl, who was walking at the end of the line of three, now four, must have realized there was an extra something in line ! Something extra and it was walking along right behind her !! Something she was sure was not suppose to be there !

Before I could say a word, she let out a scream and in one big, flying leap (I swear she never touched the water) landed in her dad's arms. He was one of the men out in the middle of the stream, walking along with the gas lantern.

After we all got done laughing, including the girl, we could not believe how far she had jumped from a standing start, into her dad's arms. It had to set a new world record.

Chapter 16

SKUNKS

Well, up here in the good ole U.P. there is one type of critter we sure do not have a shortage of, SKUNKS !! We have them all over the place! Where you least want them ! One of our main problems comes with the cool weather in the fall of the year. Mr. Skunk likes to find a nice warm place to spend the cold days of winter. Usually, for some strange reason, a person does not have a problem knowing when this action by Mr. Skunk is taking place anywhere near his home. This could mean under your porch or deck, in the garage, by your bedroom window..... The first person they always used to call when they had this unwanted, smelly, troublemaker, this wood's kitty, stop in to spend the winter was the Conservation Officer. For this reason, we have come to get acquainted with them quite well. We also get to hear a lot of skunk stories that they like to tell.

74

FLATTEN IT:

It seems that this family from town had a skunk problem. It was looking for a home and liked to hang around their house. Mr. Skunk had even made plans to set up a permanent residence near their garage. The wife of the house did not like this idea at all, for the normal reasons, but the man of the house could not find time to trap it to get rid of it. A guy up here has a lot more important things to do in the fall of the year besides trying to trap a skunk. Being an avid hunter, and not wanting the skunk to interfere with his outdoor activities, he put two and two together and comes up with a great idea:SHOOT IT!

Plans were laid out for the next time Mr. Skunk comes around their house. Now he would be ready ! Things worked out just right, along comes Mr. Skunk, he waited for just the right moment, shoots the skunk, takes it out and buries it, now this problem is solved. Just another job well done by the man of the house !

But it seems that there was one little setback !! Not everything was as it first appeared.

The next morning, being Sunday, they all went out to go to church. They got into their van that was parked in their garage and as they backed up they found they had a flat tire !

It seems that when the husband shot Mr. Skunk, it took care of the skunk problem alright, but the bullet also traveled through the garage wall and got their van tire too. Now explain yourself out of this one to the wife ! or at least try too !

HOLIDAY SPECIAL:

Well, this is a true holiday story. It seems that his older couple were going to have a lot of company over during the holiday season. So, the lady of the house made plans and went out and picked up this real big holiday turkey. Her plans were to cook this turkey up in advance so it would be one less thing to worry about when company came over. There was so much for the two of them to get done during the already busy holiday period. She cooked it up and after it was done, they cut off a few slices to test it out, to make sure it was just right. It tasted great!

She then took the roaster with the turkey in it out on her patio deck. Here she placed a large window box over the roaster that held the turkey. On top of the window box she put a heavy planter to hold things down. Everything was all set, she did not have to worry about her turkey anymore.

Sometime later she had reason to look out on her patio and saw that the planter was knocked over ! The window box had been moved, and the roaster lay off the deck on the ground. She went outside and saw off a little ways lay the skeleton of her big holiday turkey, their nice, big, all-ready-for company turkey, or what was left of it. Her husband then came out and looked around the corner of the house and there lay Mrs. Skunk that had just enjoyed his holiday feast !! In fact, so much so that he could not even get his feet under his now to fat body to get away. He had eaten the whole thing !!

The moral of the story is: Do not try to get even with those that may steal your holiday turkey, unless you are more then ready to put up with the smell !!

GUILTY:

The old time Game Wardens used to live trap the skunks that were giving the people in town problems. They would set out a live trap baited with peanut butter and jelly, a skunk would come after the peanut butter and jelly and get caught in the trap. They would sneak up with a black trash bag, putting it over the trap, to cut off all the light from the skunk. If the skunk was in complete darkness, you could put him in the trunk of your patrol car and drive him out into the woods and let him go.

The only problem we ever had was trying to sneak up on a trap that already had a skunk trapped in it, and then trying to place the black trash bag over the trap. You want to do this without really upsetting the skunk. All these times I never really ever got sprayed, but there was this time I thought I had made another successful skunk transfer. After getting done, I dropped the other officer off at his house, and I went home for lunch. As soon as I hit the door my wife said, "Get out of here ! How did you get sprayed?" Maybe our trapping adventure had not been as successful as we thought it was. Since the other officer's wife had also found him guilty by association !! After that, I took 1/4" plywood and enclosed my live traps, to have Mr. Skunk in the dark as soon as he got caught.

Chapter 17

SPEARING

Well, I have always said that in some of the areas where I worked a boy would not be allowed to wear long pants until he speared his first fish (ILLEGALLY). Also, I have always said that the worst problem with getting caught is not the fine you may have to pay, but the fact that for years to come you are going to get ribbed, every time you stop in one of the local pubs, get ready for the boys to let loose. For this reason, you have to remember that there is always the VICTIMS story of what REALLY took place, the GAME WARDEN'S story of how he really caught them, then (somewhere in the middle) maybe the real truth.

"WHO ME ?"

Up here in the Eastern part of the U.P., there is a Northern Pike spawning area called Brian Grade. There is a big marsh off the creek that comes out of Milakokia Lake where big (and I mean big!) Northern Pike come to spawn. They do this in really shallow water where it is very easy to spear them. Some of the favorite spots for pike to spawn are right next to the road. Here, people are tempted beyond what some people are capable of controlling. In fact, this area was so active in years past that the locals renamed it "Pike Grade". This is my favorite story to kind of rib a couple of the locals that got caught at Pike Grade. You see up in this area there are "clans". They work out in the woods for a living. Seeing they cut timber, they are around these spawning fish all the time. Some of them feel it is just like stopping at a grocery store on the way home from work. Self-serve type ! On the way home, you just stop to pick up a few fish or whatever game you may need for supper. It is just a way of life for them to "bend" the rules, to get a fish. BUT, does it hurt their pride when they get caught ! Now this story, is their side of how they got caught with some illegal Pike, but I do help them remember by filling in some parts that were either forgotten or just left out.

It seems that a couple of brothers from one of these U.P. clans were caught with a burlap sack full of Northern Pike at Brian (Pike) Grade. The way they tell the story things did not turn out fair for them at all. Their story goes like this: It seems that there was this youth down in the marsh spearing. He had speared a few Pike, placing them in this burlap sack. The brothers just happened to be in the area. They observed this youth having some success spearing so being the outdoor type they decided to stop and watch him. Now they were just curious to see how he did it. He was pretty good, so it brought back memories for the brothers. The brothers while day dreaming of times gone by, all of a sudden realize that the youth was gone !! The sack full of Pike lay at their feet, along with the spear. PLUS, two men in green uniforms were now standing there with them ! For some reason, bewildering to them, the Game Wardens assumed there was some connection between these two brothers and the sack of Pike. To this day, they still claim this is really the way things happened. I add a little fuel by adding the following to get them going.

These two brothers were standing near the marsh off Pike Grade. Just enjoying a nice warm spring day. Watching the pike do their thing at their feet by the water's edge. All of a sudden, out of nowhere, this youth runs up ! He yells to the brothers, "Mister, please hold this for me a minute !" He then hands them a spear and a burlap sack whose flopping contents they had no idea of. The boy then runs off back into the marsh. Right then wouldn't you know it two Game Wardens appear out of nowhere, they put two and two together and come up with, two brothers, a spear and a sack full of illegal pike !! Old stories die hard in the U.P.

OLD AGE WINS OUT:

Here in Michigan a Conservation Officer can work until they are seventy years of age. For this reason, seeing that most of the poachers you are trying to catch are in their teens and twenties, you have to come up with a better idea. If a party is standing in a stream trying to spear a trout illegally, you cannot walk up and say, "Conservation Officer, Would you step over here please ?" All you would see would be tennis shoes going off through the woods at a high rate of speed. I have always said that after forty years of age, if a Game Warden did not catch them in their first four steps, his chances were not good of ever catching them. For this reason we had to come up with ways to compensate for our short comings.

There was this older officer that worked an area where there was a lot of illegal netting for Walleye Pike while they were spawning. Now these Walleye would come right up to the shore of the lake to spawn. Walleye have a real bright red eye that glows in the dark when a light shines on it. Walleye, for this reason are real easy to spear or net. The outlaw just takes his spear and aims for the bright red eye. This particular officer was close to seventy years of age, but still real active out in the field. Since the years when he could run down a poacher had long since passed, he came up with a better idea. This officer knew this area where the poachers would be trying to take a few Walleye. So he just picked his spot and waited.

This night, sure enough, along came a couple of guys looking for fish. After they worked the spawning area for fish, one of the violators started to leave. Things were working just as this older officer planned. Our poacher that had the walleye came right up the path toward where the officer was hiding. Now, maybe tonight, he would score. Where the officer was hiding, there was this hedge row that the poacher had to go through. As the poacher passed through the hedge, the officer stood up, in the pitch dark of night, reached out and grabbed the poacher in a "Bear Hug" !! at the same time telling him he was a Game Warden. Our poacher, in his mid-twenties, just started to scream at the top of his lungs from fright !! Finally, he realized who had hold of him. He recognized the Game Warden and settled down. They were both from a town of a couple of hundred people so really knew each other. He then told the officer, "I spent a couple of tours over in Vietnam, but even with that I have never been scared like I was tonight ! When those arms came out of the dark to encircle my body, I thought I would die !"

LEARNING FROM YOUR ELDERS:

One night, I received a call from the State Police Post. Their patrol car had just stopped a car with a well know poacher in it. The car was in the area of Indian Lake, where the Walleye were spawning, and the party just stunk of fish. BUT no fish !!

I put my uniform on and got into my patrol car to go out. I looked over the spawning area without finding anything. I did find a spot where someone had walked across the golf course in the dew. But nothing else. I parked there and spent a couple of hours watching the area of the golf course waiting for them to come back for their illegal fish. No luck.

ALL OF A SUDDEN IT DAWNED ON ME !!

The old timers (Game Wardens) had always said that the walleye spawn right after dark, up until about midnight. I put two and two together to figure out that this party had already taken his Walleye illegally and was on his way home when he got stopped by the state police patrol car ! I had been working on the wrong end of the crime for the last couple of hours ! There had been no fish in his car when he was stopped, but he had sure smelled of fish. Putting this together, I figured he had hid the fish before being stopped. It was now about 2:30 a.m., so I went home for a couple of hours of sleep. I then got up before daylight to head out to Indian lake. The walleye had to be between the lake and where his car had been stopped. On my way, just a mile or so from town, I passed our poacher that the state police had stopped the night before heading back for town. I quickly turned around to stop him. When the party pulled over, I told him why I had stopped him, then told him to head for the State Police Post, and I would follow him.

At the State Police Post we obtained a search warrant for the car. In the truck, we found seventy walleye that had been speared illegally.

You see, it does pay to listen to those old timers that have been through the mill a couple of dozen times before you ever came along.

Chapter 18

GOD'S COUNTRY - MICHIGAN'S U.P.

As I said in the forward of this book, I grew up in Michigan's upper peninsula. The U.P. as it is rightly called. Now there just may be a few of you out there that are having a hard time trying to figure out just where the U.P. is. What kind of people make it up, and how they really make do. Someone asked my daughter at work one day how old I was, because he had been reading my stories in the paper. She told him that I was in my forties. The party stated that I could not be with the stories I told and when they had to have taken place ! I am. But you must remember that before TV the U.P. was a good thirty years behind the rest of the world. Now with the aid of TV, we have cut that in half. Back when I was in school, if the town had a good basketball team that was playing an away game all the stores in town closed so they could go to the game. Everyone went ! It was the only entertainment there was in town during the winter. During summer, playing "kick-the-can" was the prime-time neighborhood activity. You just waited for the day you got old enough to play with the big kids. Then you were "in". The real sign of manhood was going to school with an old small game license pinned to an old hand-me-down plaid hunting coat. It really did not matter how many holes were worn in it before it ever got to you.

Going through some of my Mom's things I came across these facts someone printed about the U.P.

From parts of the U.P., you are closer to nine states and one foreign country than you are to the state capital. Ask a person in the U.P. their nationality and more will claim to be Finnish or Swedish than American.

In places you can drive for 150 miles without finding a stop light.

Two break-ins are considered a crime wave

With Hardee's or McDonald's announcing a new restaurant it is front page news.

You could miss Summer if you sleep in late.

People are more concerned with the spring smelt (fish) runs, than how their legislator voted.

A ten percent unemployment rate is low.

You're not "weird" if you smile at a stranger.

Rapid transit is a bunch of snowmobilers going from one town to another.

It takes at least twenty years to qualify as a resident.

You must fly South to go North.

You're related to someone.

You're nobody if you don't have a nickname.

More money is won or lost at bingo than on the stock market.

You always hear someone say, "Whuh hy"

The water is not warm enough to swim in till August if then.

The State Highway Department closes it's rest areas in October and does not open them till May.

You're nothing if you don't own a 4x4 pickup with a plow.

You can pry copper souvenirs out of some of the old roads.

You work your social calendar around the schedules of the high school basketball and hockey teams.

People always tell you how terrible the winters are, but don't answer when you ask why they still live here.

Coke is still a soft drink.

People from "down-state" have nicknames like trolls, sugar-beaters, fudgies, etc.

There are still a number of counties with under 10.000 people.

There were a number of others on the list , but these few kind of let you know where the U.P. is and the type of people that make it their home. It's just a special kind of place.

CHAPTER 19

CHRISTMAS IN THE U.P.

Well, it sure looks like we will have a white Christmas again this year. Up here in the U.P., the odds are very good that we will. In fact, growing up over in Ontonagon, we used to wish and wonder if we would ever have a green one! We never did. It seems so funny, sitting here now, thinking back on those "good old days". Back then a family was a family, a home was truly a home, there were not any televisions to let us know about the rest of the world. What they were doing or what they thought. In fact, usually during the day, you were lucky to pick up a good radio station you could hear clearly. At night, when the big stations turned up their power, you could only lay there and dream about where they really might be located at. How far were they from Ontonagon in the U.P.? You could listen to all the old, real great radio-talk shows. For instance "Sky King", Bobby Bensen and the B/B Riders", "The Shadow", "Straight Arrow", and on and on. Boy, those were the nights when a young boys mind would have to fill in the pictures to what he was listening too.

Our real world was built around our family and friends around our little U.P. town. To go to Grandma's house sixty mile away was called a vacation. Now we travel that far to just eat supper, then come back home. You never worried about what others may have had that you did not, because you never knew what you were missing out on. There was never, back in the "good old days", all the negative news about how bad Christmas was going to be, or how poor the poor people were, or how cold and awful the winter was going to be.

For this was the U.P., and half those things were a normal way of life up here.

Now, let's take a few of those overpaid, negative-minded, prime-time, newsmen back, to Ontonagon for a Christmas a "few" years ago, during the "good old days".

Man, those were the days that will forever stick in a persons mind, and be as real as a picture as I sit here thinking about them.

Now back then, we kids thought that our Mom and dad were special.

They never told us the bad news. They never told us the paper mill where Dad worked was to shut down, the bills had added up, or that things were going to be real rough this year. All that we knew was that it was going to be another special year. You see, the paper mill where my dad worked shut down overnight with no warning to the workers. Up there, back then it was the only place to work. Years later, the White Pine copper mines opened up, but until then things were rough. We had to pull together as a family. All of us, with Mom's help, delivered every Sunday newspaper in town so we could make the five cents a paper they paid, to be put in the family kitty. During the summer month, all the kids and Mom would pick Nightcrawlers all night long after a good rain. They were sold to help the family out and pay bills. Pennies, dimes, nickels were saved. Life back then was a family project.

Come the fall of the year, Mom would get out her knitting needles and start on her Christmas projects. She could talk and keep knitting, help with our schoolwork and keep knitting, catch us doing what we weren't suppose to and keep knitting, all this time never missing a stitch in what she was making. She would spend time down at the Co-op Store trying to match flour sacks for special things for her kids, My Grandpa Walker was a woods worker, who in his spare time had perfected the art of whittling toys for the grand kids. I still have a little fish tug that he whittled for me over forty years ago. Back then things were truly hand-made. You see, since years before my Dad and Grandpa drove a steam engine (train) for the logging camps, there was no better present for a boy than a hand-made model of their steam engine, just like the real one they used to operate. I still have this too, with a few missing wheels that got wore off. My other Grandpa owned a wood working shop, so he too, added to our booty.

Back in those days, most of the kids in town belonged to 4-H Clubs. Here we would learn crafts. Then we would make projects for each other for Christmas. After Mom died, I found an old ash tray that I had made for Dad, using free Lake Superior rocks and plaster in her bedroom chest. A treasure she held onto for forty years. It sure was hard to keep your projects a secret, when all the kids went to the same 4-H Club. But leading into the Christmas season this was our social life in the U.P.

As I stated before, I still have some of these hand-made artifacts. These gifts that could only be special to a Mom or Dad from one of their kids. Now back to me after forty years. These gifts were made from the heart of a kid and could never be important to anyone but me today.

About a month before Christmas, Mom would start her Christmas baking. She made all kinds of special treats for her kids, and half the town. You see, you shared what you had back then with those around you. It sure was not hard to snitch, but these items were stored in the freezer (the unheated back porch, nobody had a real freezer back then). Mom, she knew what each of us kids thought was really special to eat. Mine was Gumdrop cake and raisin cookies! You could bet that come Christmas day, no matter how bad times may be, you would at least get a treat of some of what you liked. These goodies were made as only a mom could make them.

All things were working out, we were getting close to Christmas day. Soon that special morning, the night before you put out a few of your favorite cookies and a glass of milk for you-know-who! Then, we were off to bed but not to sleep.

Now it was Christmas morning in the U.P. All of us kids would get each other up. We would sit on the top of the stairs that led down into the living room. We could not go down until everyone was ready. Dad would always pretend that he was just too tired to get out of bed, just to make us suffer a little. We would beg and beg him to get up! We would finally talk him into getting up. Dad would always go down first, check the fire, then put on some Christmas music (an old 78 speed record.) Then and only then, would we kids get called down into the living room. The waiting was a form of child brutality back then, but we loved it. Now it was here, finally!! The planning that had led up to Christmas morning had built up so much excitement in us that it was unreal. Christmas was here and all the guessing would soon be over, so off we went.

From Grandpa was another home made toy and maybe even more then one. Wow! From Mom, there were the "hunting" socks, plus mittens she had knit, and look a scarf (that no red-blooded, All American boy would be caught dead wearing). Boy, look here! The mittens have a slit in them, so you can stick out your trigger finger to shoot your Red Ryder BB gun without taking the mittens off. Just like Dad's. There were oranges, candy, apples and a few nuts in your stocking that Grandma and Grandpa had sent over. Dad always had something special for each kid. There was always one thing from him and Mom each year, no matter how hard it may have been to get it. Boy, what a day, and it had only started.

For on this day, Dad always bought a package of link sausage. Now you have to remember, back in those days, only on Christmas morning did you have pancakes, eggs, and Dad's special gift of link sausage. (All the rest of the year, breakfast was oatmeal or lumpy cream of wheat!) Boy, you were on a roll, with all the gifts, and a breakfast of your dreams to eat! Wow! What a day already!! Why? Because Mom and dad made the day what it was, not the build-up of TV or being down from hearing how bad things were. How could things be bad? You had Grandparents, a Mom and dad, and a family that loved you, enough to give you all these special, personally-made, just for you, presents. Boy! Life was great.

Besides, you know Christmas would be great. because you checked as you came by the kitchen door. One glance at the kitchen table where you had left the milk and cookies for "you-know-who," and you saw that the cookies were gone. Plus, the milk glass was empty! So, you knew he had been here.

Chapter 20

WIFEE

You know, to really be an avid hunter and get away with it, you do have to have an understanding wife (wifee). But, even if you have a wife that understands, there will still be times she does not.

BUT YOU DON'T UNDERSTAND:

Sitting here thinking about hunting and fishing, really brings to mind how easy it is for some of us men to be really mis-under-stood. Did you really ever stop to think of what us poor hunters have to put up with ? How it can effect us ? Right away, a couple things come to mind.

First of all, a guy will be sitting in his easy chair. Tired, trying to relax. Reading the back part of the sport section, pages where they warn you about all the crazy ideas they are dreaming up down in the state capital (Lansing). Now down there is where they collect all the ideas from all over the state. Then, they try and make them into one rule for us hunters to try to figure out and obey. If you stop to and think about them, you are already in trouble.

Here you are, with your mind 300 miles away, down in the "big house" in Lansing, trying to think like they do down there, again you are in trouble for all of a sudden, you realize that your wife has been standing there talking to you ! All you hear from her are the last two words she spoke ! These last two words, all by themselves, do not make a whole lot of sense. But, the worst part of it is that your wife is not talking anymore. By the look on her face, you can tell she is waiting for an answer. So putting your best foot forward, as best as you know how, you try to give her an intelligent answer based on those last two words you heard her speak. The only, two words you heard. Then, by the look on her face now, you realize that there must have been something lost in the translation. Then you hear, "Honey, you never pay any attention to me, anymore !" You do, honest ! But she does not understand your mind was not here in Manistique at home, But 300 miles to the south, down in the "big house" going over next year's hunting rules. Now this whole problem with your wife was not your fault, but theirs, if only they would leave things alone.

DEER (DEAR) PROBLEMS:

Now there is this other time, you're sitting in the kitchen drinking a cup of coffee. But really, your mind is out in your deer blind. You are thinking about that nice 8-point buck that came into your blind from your off-side. In order to get a shot at it, you had to try to turn all the way around. Needless to say you were not successful. So here you are sitting at your kitchen table, but really you are out in your deer blind. In your mind is this nice buck again, but this time you have moved your blind over a little, making plans for next year. Yup ! next year things will be different !! You won't miss that nice 8-pointer again ! He won't get away this time. The more you think about the dumb move you made there last year that cost you a shot at this buck, the madder you get, after all it was all your fault, you just moved to fast. Plus the blind was set up the wrong way.

All of a sudden you hear, "Honey, what are you thinking about ?" Without thinking you say, "Nothing". How in the world do you tell your wife, "Honey, I'm not really here. You know that big buck I missed last deer season ? Well, it sure won't happen next year, seeing I was just out in my deer blind, while sitting at the kitchen table, making plans". For some reason you think your wife may think you are nuts after hearing your story and she just may be able to prove it. Now, she says, "Your mad about something. I can see it on your face." You answer, "No I'm not." "I can tell you are ! What were you thinking about ?" "Nothing !" (Really I think we passed this spot a few minutes back !) Can you believe it ? That stupid deer is still causing problems, almost two month after the close of deer season !!

There's also the time, you give a good answer to a question, from a sportsmen point of view, you still get in trouble. I was up in the courthouse one day, gabbing in the coffee room. There is a problem with me being understood at times, when I put my answers into good old U.P. laymen terms. No matter how hard I try to use examples that the average person should be able to understand without any problem, there is at times a problem with them being understood.

Now here we sit, but to get the situation in the proper perspective, you have to understand the following. I have had the same wife, the only one, for over a quarter of a century. So I try to explain to the girls at the courthouse, using an example of how life really is, using one of my better illustrations and they will say, "We don't know how your wife puts up with you." They don't understand that to know me is to love me ! Let me give you an example about how using a sportsmen illustration can get you in real trouble.

A DOG'S LIFE:

One day, while waiting for a jury to return a verdict, we were sitting in the coffee room. The subject of divorce came up. They asked me about it. Now having had only one wife and planning to keep it that way, I told them this story.

A sportsman has a good hunting dog. It hunts good, has a great personality, behaves in the car and around the house, is good with the kids and is his best buddy. Face it, this dog is tops, number one in the hunters mind. He would not sell it for a million dollars. (Old Rocky is just as special and this)! Now say Rocky was to get hit by a car or lost while hunting and you could not find him. Now you are without a hunting buddy.

Chances are this hunter would look around and go through a dozen dogs before he ever found one to replace the one he had lost. It would really be hard to replace old Rocky. You would need one that hunts as good, is great around the kids and the house, and just a super good dog, plus Rocky was just special after all those years together.. I then told them, "I feel the same way about my wife. She is really special. I could never find someone else to treat me as she does, so I'll just keep her around. Besides I know guys that have had to go through a dozen different ones before they ever found one as good as the one they got rid of. It's kind of like having a good hunting dog, stick with the one that will hunt, why take a chance that the next one won't !! Something was lost in the interpretation, the girls threw me out of the coffee room.

Chapter 21

HUNTER'S WISDOM

GOOD-DEAL'S:

Now, it takes a long time and a lot of training to come up with a sportsman's mentality. I am sure that there are those out there that still have their doubts as to whether we, sportsmen, have a mentality at all; but we true lovers of the great outdoors have to be on our toes all the time. Unless when we are not we could miss out on something great.

The following falls under the category, "Did you ever ?"

Now I would hate to think that I am the only one that ever....

Did you ever run across something that you were not really looking for while in a sporting goods section of a store ? But then it is just to good of a deal to pass up ? It seems that there is this little problem that a lot of hunters and fishermen have... But I am getting ahead of myself.

This is how it happens when you go into those big mall type stores. As you walk around you have to keep a sharp eye out for those big, bright orange signs that say "CLEARANCE"!!! There has to be a reason they always seem to be colored "hunter's Orange. That is to attract hunters, right ?

Now I go into this mall type store and into the sporting goods section. Then with all my years and training as a Game Warden, I look around to spot these hunters orange signs. I can spot them half-way across a store. I rush to get over there before any other hunter can make his move. As usual, now there seems like there are some really good deals on the shelf today. Those deals that other sportsmen have just not had a chance to take advantage of yet. The price is always marked way down on these items, so low you feel kind of guilty buying them. But your timing has to be just right before some other smart sportsmen comes across them. Looking them over you find a few that you would have to be checked out mentally for if you did not take advantage of at this price. You could not live with yourself if you just walked away and all next hunting season you would think of the great deal you missed out on. Let me give you a couple of examples of how this sportsmen mentality works.

I was in a store the other day and then ended up in one of these sporting goods clearance areas. It was a dream come true !! Shotgun shells, steel shot, 12 gauge shells, 60% off !! These were name brand, 12 gauge magnum shells, waterfowl steel shot, 3" steel shot at that: at 60% off. There is no way a waterfowl hunter could pass by a deal like this, so I bought both boxes for next to nothing. 3" steel shot for this price, unheard of !! Now this is the second year in a row that I have come across this type of steal-deal on boxes of 3" steel shot waterfowl shells. So now I have five boxes of 3" steel shot waterfowl shells. There is only one slight problem that I now have to face. That is, that I do not own a shotgun that will shoot a 3" shell. But I do hope to some day, so thinking ahead and planning for the future, I just had to buy them.

NOTHING VENTURED, NOTHING GAINED:

Then there was this other day. This time it was really all my wife's fault for needing some material. I, again, landed under one of those bright hunter's orange signs that read clearance. On this day they really had some good deals. They had all those attachments for a compound bow for 50% off !! Now I do own a compound bow ! I'm not that dumb ! So I took advantage of a couple of these really great deals. I bought a number of those "add-on" attachments that are suppose to improve your hunting ability. Now I do need some help in improving my hitting ability while out bow hunting, so it seems like a good deal at 50% off. The problems started when I got the "good deals" home.

I spent hours trying to figure out how these gadgets worked ! I could not get them to work no matter what I did, or on the back of it, it said, "to use gadget number "3" you also must buy gadget number "5". Now you have to understand that gadget number "5" was not on sale. Also it could not be found anywhere in the U.P. even at full price. So still knowing a real good deal when I saw it, I wrapped up item "3" for a Christmas present and gave it to my young hunting buddy as a gift. After all, starting out at his young age, he has a lot more years than I do to figure out how it works.

P.S. Two year and two bow seasons later item number "3" is still sitting on a shelf in his parents kitchen.

BETTER LATE THAN NEVER:

Then there was another time that I needed all the items that you use along with your black powder muzzle loader for deer hunting. I went out and at top price bought a flask, powder gauge, primers, etc.. I was scared to tell my wife how much all these items bought one by one cost. My only hope was she had found some "good deals" over in the sewing section and felt the same way I did.

Well, two weeks later I am back in one of those mall stores. I wander over under the now famous bright hunters orange sign that read clearance in the sporting goods section. But by now after some of my other really good deals I am a lot smarter, right ? But right under this clearance sign I find some black powder kits. These kits have all the needed equipment: flask, powder gauge, primers, balls (wrongs caliber), etc. in a little plastic case. These equipment cases, loaded with all these items, are marked down from $60.00 to just $13.00 !! Can you believe it ?? Now I cannot figure out how much of a percentage I am saving, for this deal is just too mind boggling to take the time to figure out. Here sits ! not one ! but two kits at $13.00 each !! What a deal ! Mrs. Walker did not raise any dummy! So I really took advantage of that store ! I bought both of them. I figured I could throw half the kit away and still come out a winner.

Well, you never know, maybe one of your buddies will lose his kit and need one, or just maybe-someday, your grand kids will want to go black powder hunting with grandpa. See ? there are always really good deals with valid reasons why a sportsman should take advantage of them and be wrong if he passed them up.

By the way does anyone have a 12 gauge shot gun, that shoots "3" inch shells that they want to sell ?

BACKWOODS GLOSSARY

Up here in the Great North Woods, there is a tendency to use terms or phrases to make a point. To some of you, they may be used in a way you never realized they could be. Other words or terms, you may just have not had the opportunity to ever use. This Backwoods Glossary is to help you out in understanding why we talk like we do.

U.P. (Upper Michigan): If, for some strange reason, you have never traveled in Michigan, these two letters would seem strange to you. First, understand that Michigan has two peninsulas- the upper and lower. The lower peninsula is made up of two parts, Lower Michigan and Northern Michigan. But, the really important part of Michigan lies across the Mackinac Bridge. This part of Michigan is called the U.P., for the Upper peninsula of Michigan. The people up here in the U.P. live in their own little world and like it that way. The only problem is that most of the laws are passed down in Lower Michigan to correct their problems, then they effect us, who may not even be part of that problem. Some of the Big City folks that pass these laws never have learned to understand and love the U.P. like we that live here do. The natives of the U.P. have trouble understanding the "why-for" about some of these laws, therefore they feel they really must not apply to them.

Two of the biggest industries in the U.P. are paper mills and the men that work in the woods suppling trees to these mills so they can produce their product. There are probably more colleges in the U.P., per capita, than anywhere else in the country. But even with this, there are still a lot of natives up here that feel you could sure ruin a good person if you sent them to one of these colleges. News of a serious crime will travel from one side of the U.P. to the other like a wild fire. Because most people up here are not used to it. To them, serious crimes are when someone takes a deer or some fish illegally and is dumb enough to get caught. They don't even take these crimes to seriously unless the poacher should step over the line and get to greedy.

Sports teams that play teams from other towns in the U.P. always seem to have relatives, or friends, on the other team. Everyone knows someone, or someone that married someone, that knew someone from over there. To win a state championship, you have to beat those teams from "down state". To do this is a dream come true for any red-blooded U.P. boy or girl.

When I was growing up, we had only had part-time radios. So we had to be Green Bay (Wisconsin) Packer and Milwaukee Brave fans. As a boy living in the Western U.P., we could not pick up any radio stations that carried broadcast of the teams from Lower Michigan. For this reason, we grew up feeling that we were a state unto ourselves. We could not be part of Michigan, because it was just to far away, and the only way to get there was by boat. We knew we were not part of Wisconsin, so we were just the Good Old U.P.!

Up her in the U.P., where life is tough, but things are good, and it is just a great place to live.

Some backwoods (U.P.) terms:

2-TRACK:(roads)

The U.P. has hundreds of miles of this type of road. All these roads consist of are two tire ruts worn into the ground from all the vehicle travel throughout the years. Usually you have a high, grass-covered center and mud holes in the low spots. This is one of the reasons that so many people in the U.P. feel you cannot live without a 4x4 pickup. These roads are never worked on or improved and you get what you see.

Blacktop Roads:

These are the 2-tracks, that are worse than unimproved roads. They are covered by mud or clay and it is a real trick to stay between the trees on some of these. There are also a lot of these type roads for which the U.P. is famous. Many a fishermen or hunter has spent hours and hours trying to get out of one of these blacktop roads, usually after you misjudged what you were getting into. Two of the first things I learned after becoming a Game Warden stationed in the U.P. were: It's hard to get 2-ton stuck at fifty miles an hour, so wind it up and keep moving. The other one follows point one, you are never really stuck till you stop. In other words, if one of these blacktop areas sneak up on you, floor it and don't stop 'til you reach high ground or hit something unmovable.

Poachers:

These are not people that cook eggs in hot water, but may get themselves in hot water now and then. They are outlaws that rob the honest hunters and fishermen of their chance to get game and fish legally. In years past, it was a way of life in the U.P. that was passed down from generation to generation. When it was an accepted thing to do, the Game Warden not only had a hard time catching the poachers, but he usually had an even harder time trying to get a conviction in the local courts.

Shining:

(Shinning, Shining, Shiners), Shiners are the poachers that use a spotlight to look for deer at night, in order to shoot them. Until the fines got to high, it was the way that a lot of the outlaws did their hunting here in the U.P. They would take a pair of spotlights, hook them up in their vehicle, then drive around while casting the rays of the spotlights out into fields or an old orchards, until they spotted a deer. The deer, blinded by the bright light, would stand there staring at the light while the poacher got out his gun and shot it. There is really no sport in it, because it is so deadly. You will notice I spelled shinning, with two "n's" at times. Well, I did this on my tickets for dozens of cases throughout the years, until a State Trooper told me it was spelled wrong. He said it should only have one "n", so on the next couple tickets I changed how I spelled shining. You see for years, when I caught someone hunting deer at night with a spotlight, the only thing I would write for a charge on the ticket was the one word "shinning". With the one word spelled, Shinning, they knew what they did, I knew what they had done, and most important the average U.P. Judge knew what they were standing before him for doing. Well, the first time I caught a crew out spotlighting for deer and put shining (with one n) on their ticket they pled "Not Guilty". They must have been confused by the spelling and so was I.

Spearers:

These are people that have a way of taking fish with the use of a spear. The spear can have from three to five prongs, with pointed tips, these prongs have barbs on the end to hold the fish on the spear after they spear it. Now in some areas, it is legal to spear certain types of non-game fish. The problem the Game Warden has is with those that spear trout, salmon, walleye, etc. or "game fish". When these fish come into real shallow water to spawn, a Game Warden will spend hour after hour watching the fish spawning in these areas.

Extractors:

This is a term for those illegal fishermen that may come a long a creek with a spear trying to extract the spawning fish from the creek. They may use other devices besides a spear. For instance a weighted hook, hand nets, their hands, etc.

Gill Netters:

These are people, both legal and illegal, that use a gill net to take fish. In some areas, there is a commercial fishery allowed with the use of gill nets, but in Michigan it is never legal for "sport" fishermen to use a gill net to take fish. A gill net is made up of nylon string in little squares (it looks something little a small woven wire fence) built so the fish will swim into the net putting their head through the square openings. Then, they get caught when their larger body will not fit through the squares and their gills keep them from backing out of the nets. I have observed illegal gill net fishermen take hundreds of pounds of steelhead in a couple of hours, if they set their gill nets in the right spot.

Fishhouse or fishshed:

In areas of the U.P., along the great lakes where there is a legal commercial fishery, most of those business involved have a building where they clean, box in ice, and store their catch. They may also repair their nets in this building. On account of the smell around a full time commercial fishing operation, most of these sheds are located away from any residence. They also may be on the river bank where the commercial fisherman ties up his fish tug. For this reason they are often used for illegal activity, sometimes by others than those that own them.

Deer camp:

A deer camp can be any type of building used for offering protection from the elements. It is also used to "get-a-way from home during the hunting season. Some are as nice as any house, better than some, while others may be made out of plastic, heavy paper, scrap lumber, or anything to keep the weather out. The following rules are some of the usual type that are proper for deer camp life.

(1)You cannot shave or take a bath, no matter how many days you may be staying at camp. You are allowed to wash your face and hands. But this is your own choice, You do not have to if you do not want to. This is one reason young boys love to go to deer camp with Dad.

(2)There is no proper way to dress while at deer camp, if it feels good wear it ! You can even wear the same clothes all week long. This includes your socks, if you can catch them after the first three days at camp.

(3)The "menu" is always made up of all the "proper" things that you cannot afford to eat all the rest of the year at home. Both good and bad for you.

(4)It is never wrong to tell a "true" story on another camp member. Remembering it is of more value if you can dress it up a little to make him suffer all the time you are telling it. During the telling of his misfortune we must all remember that we will all pay for our mistakes, sooner or later, if and when our hunting "buddies" find out about them.

(5)It is a crime, punishable by banishment, to talk about school, or school work, or any work for that matter while at deer camp.

(6)You can throw, hang or just leave your socks and clothes any where they land when you remove them. You can hang your wet socks from anything that has something to hang them from to try and dry them out before the next days hunt. Always remembering it is "most" important to have dry socks by daybreak the next morning.

(7)What may be called work at home is not work at deer camp. Therefore getting things done at deer camp is not classified as work, but a team effort. For this reason, it is not wrong for a boy to do dishes, sweep a floor, pick up trash (that he missed getting in the trash can when he threw it that way, with one of his famous hook shots), or even do what Dad asks him to do, the first time Dad asks him to do it.

You would have to spend a week at a real U.P. deer camp to really know the true feeling of being a U.P. deer hunter. With these easy-to-apply rules, you can see why deer camp life is so important to a boy during his informative teenage years. It is really important that a young man start out with a proper perspective on life.

Big House:

This is the Michigan State Capital, from some areas of the U.P. it can be over 400 miles away. In Lansing, this is where "they" compile all the rules and ideas that are put out to confuse the average hunter or fisherman, while out in the field. It is the feeling of a lot of U.P. sportsmen, that most of those that work down there, in Lansing's Big House, never in their lives set foot in the real out-of-doors, or wet a line in a back woods stream. What they know, they got from someone that wrote a book without ever having set their feet in a real woods, or having gone back woods fishing either. It is just passed on from desk to desk, year after year, put into volumes of rules and law books that we out in the field have to learn to live with. This while trying to enjoy ourselves out in the real Northwoods, the U.P.

Wifee:

(W-IF-EE; wify) This is one's wife. To pronounce it right, you say the "W" sound, then the "IF", than draw out the "EE".

Big Lake:

This can be any of the Great Lakes that border Michigan. Instead of saying, " I went fishing out on Lake Michigan Saturday". A native from the U.P. would say, "I went fishing on the Big Lake Saturday afternoon".

Off road vehicles:

ATV'S, ORV'S, dirt bikes, etc. These may be any of the type vehicles that are made primary to operate off a improved road. Some may be home made, while other are sold by dealers. In the U.P. you will find a lot of these used by sportsmen to get around when hunting and fishing.

Game Wardens:

Conservation Officer, C.O.'s, and Game Wardens are all one and the same, up here in the U.P. They have been around for better than 100 years serving the people of Michigan. The stories they can tell and those told on them are told over and over around the U.P. This is how my newspaper, story telling got started.